CITIES AND PLANNING
IN THE ANCIENT NEAR EAST

PLANNING AND CITIES

PLANNING AND CITIES

General Editor

GEORGE R. COLLINS, Columbia University

CITIES AND PLANNING IN
THE ANCIENT NEAR EAST

PAUL LAMPL

GEORGE BRAZILLER NEW YORK

TO HANSI

© 1968 George Braziller, except in U.S.
All rights reserved
For information address the publisher:
George Braziller, Inc.   One Park Avenue   New York, N.Y. 10016
Library of Congress Catalog Card Number: 68–24699
Designed by Jennie Bush
Printed in the Netherlands
First Printing

CONTENTS

PREFACE

A great number of books have been written on the art and architecture of the ancient Near East. But in spite of the paramount role cities played in the civilizations of this area, they have not yet been the subject of the ancient Near East. But in spite of the paramount role cities remains of individual cities, often tracing their vicissitudes through many centuries, mostly in a limited area. Nowhere has the exploration been as systematic and complete as in Palestine, because of interest in the biblical accounts, so that a good comparison of its cities according to their relative strata has been made possible and a clear picture of their historical development obtained. Material from literary and documentary sources has greatly added to the insight gained by archaeological evidence and has enabled scholars to study the role of the cities in the religious, economic, social, political and military history of their respective countries, mainly in specialized treatises. This book will attempt to give a comprehensive survey of the cities and of planning in the countries of the ancient Near East, albeit necessarily in a concise form.

"Planning" in this context is defined as the disposition and organization of structures and open spaces according to a conceptual order following pre-established rules of function, ritual, or aesthetics. "Cities" in the ancient Near East are defined as large, permanently settled, organized communities of people bound together by religious, political and economic interests, complementary and interdependent through a division of labor and stratification of society and headed by a priest, governor, prince or king, with a temple compound as a religious, and a palace or citadel as a political center. These cities, more often than not, were surrounded by ramparts for protection.

The unprecise term "Near East," which can denote various geographical regions, is used to comprise Asia Minor, Southwestern Asia (exclusive of the Arabian Peninsula) and Egypt.

Different geographical and climatic conditions helped to bring about a distinct development among the countries of the Near East, and any attempt by a great power to transgress these natural boundaries collapsed in due course. The natural geographical divisions which the chapters of this book follow—Mesopotamia, Egypt, the Levant, Anatolia, Armenia and Persia—became also natural political divisions in antiquity as today, though subdivisions within smaller regional confines occurred at all times.

INTRODUCTION

THE IDEA AND THE IMAGE OF THE CITY
IN THE ANCIENT NEAR EAST

Before looking back a few thousand years on the cities of the ancient
Near East from the necessarily distorted perspective of our time, it might
be appropriate to let the people of those long past days speak for themselves about what their cities meant to them.

The city appeared as such a wondrously complex and complete
organism that only a god could have created it. This legendary origin of
cities can be found in the literature of Egypt and Mesopotamia. In the
theology of Memphis (7th century B. C., based on a text more than two
thousand years older) we read:

> ...and so Ptah was satisfied, after he had made everything as well as
> all the divine order. He had formed the gods, he had made cities, he had
> founded nomes. He had put the gods in their shrines...
>
> ANET, 4–5

In a Ramesside poem (XIX Dynasty, c. 1304–1200) in praise of
Amun, Thebes (Waset) was linked "as the mistress of every city" to
Amun as the Universal God.

> He it was who existed at the beginning, from whom even the primordial
> gods sprang. To him all nations sent tribute... Waset is the pattern for
> every city. Both the flood and the earth were in her from the beginning of
> time... then mankind came into being within her, to found every city in
> her true name. Since, all are called "city" after the example of Waset.
>
> Nims, *Thebes,* 69

Ramses' capital is praised as follows:

> I have reached Per-Ramses and have found it in very good condition, a
> beautiful district without its like, after the pattern of Thebes. It was Re
> himself who founded it.
>
> (XIX Dynasty) ANET, 470–471

On a fragment of a Sumerian tablet (beginning of Second Millennium) dealing with the story of the Flood, we read about the activities
of a deity:

> after the... of kingship had been lowered from heaven... he perfected
> the rites and exalted divine laws... founded the five cities in pure places,
> called their names, apportioned them as cult centers.
>
> Kramer, *History,* 151

In a Babylonian cosmogony (6th century B.C.) from Sippar, the god
Marduk is the creator.

> The house he built, the city he built... Nippur he built, Ekur he built,
> Uruk he built, Eanna he built...
>
> Heidel, *Babylonian Genesis,* 63

7

In the Bible, though, it is man only who builds cities. In Genesis 4:16–17:

> Cain went out from the presence of the Lord and dwelt in the land of Nod on the East of Eden... and he built a city, and called the name of the city after the name of his son, Enoch...

In Genesis 10:11:

> Out of that land went forth Asshur and built Nineveh and the cities of Rechoboth and Calah.

And in Genesis 11:4 we read:

> And it came to pass as they journeyed to the East that they found a plain in the land of Shinar and they dwelt there... and they said, "Come, let us build us a city, and a tower the top of which may reach unto heaven; and let us make ourselves a name, lest we be scattered upon the face of the whole earth..."

Cities come into being by an act of God or man. According to the ideal concept of the peoples in the ancient East, cities did not develop in slow growth, To paraphrase the cosmogony: There was a time when the city had not been made... and then the city was made. The vision of a city with a tower reaching into heaven to make a name for the inhabitants is a beautiful image of the Sumerian city-state with its sky-high ziggurat (Fig. 1), vying with its neighbors for fame and supremacy, comparable to the medieval cities dominating the countryside with their cathedrals.

The Bible also gives a good glimpse of the main features of the Canaanite cities:

> Cities are great and fortified up to Heaven
>
> (Deuteronomy 1:28)

and,

> fortified cities with high walls, gates and bolts
>
> (Deuteronomy 3:5)

and we learn as well about the regional setting of the Canaanite and Israelite cities. In Judges 1:27 we read about

> Beth-shan and her dependencies, Taanach and her dependencies, Megiddo and her dependencies;

and in Joshua 18:27,

> 14 cities with their farmsteads

and in Numbers 35:3–5,

> and the cities shall serve them (the Levites) to dwell in, and their open grounds around shall be for their cattle, and for their property and for all their beasts.

What the Sumerians looked for in their cities becomes beautifully manifest in their poetry: A myth about the Moon God Nanna starts with an ideal vision of Nippur (beginning of Second Millennium):

Behold the bond of Heaven and Earth, the city...
Behold Nippur, the city...
Behold the kindly wall, the city...
Behold the Idsalla, its pure river
Behold the Karkurunna, its quay
Behold the Karasarra, its quay where the boats stand
Behold the Pulal, its well of good water
Behold the Idnunbirdu, its pure canal...

Kramer, Sumerian Mythology, 43

In a myth of the God Enki (beginning of Second Millennium) the paradisical land of Dilmun is described:

Her city drinks the water of abundance
Dilmun drinks the water of abundance
Her wells of bitter water, behold they are become wells
of good water
Her fields and farms produced crops and grains
Her city, behold, it has become the house of the
banks and quays of the land...

Kramer, Sumerian Mythology, 55

In addition to water, the city walls and the sacred precinct were the pride of the Sumerian city, expressed in the Gilgamesh epic as follows (old Babylonian version, Second Millennium):

Of ramparted Uruk the wall he built.
Of hallowed Eanna, the pure sanctuary.
Behold its outer wall, whose cornice is like copper.
Peer at the inner wall, which none can equal!
Seize upon the threshold which is of old!
Draw near to Eanna the dwelling of Ishtar
Which no future king, no man, can equal.
Go up and walk on the walls of Uruk,
Inspect the base terrace, examine the brickwork:
Is it not brickwork of burnt brick?
Did not the "Seven Sages" lay its foundation?

ANET, 72–79

Some more prosaic features of the city are referred to in the "Curse of Ereshkigal," Lady of the Underworld:

The food of the city's gutters shall be thy food; the sewers of the city shall be thy drink; the shadow of the wall shall be thy station; the threshold shall be thy habitation.

(beginning of Second Millennium)
ANET, 106–109

Since the beginning of recorded history, both written and pictorial, the tragic role of the city in a continuous cycle of life and death, of construction and destruction, is a main theme in its portrayal. The city as a symbol of civic and royal pride, as well as the actual seat of wealth and power, stands in the center of an unending struggle for and against political domination. In the annals of every land of the ancient Near East, kings and heads of state boast as much about the creation of their own cities as about the annihilation of conquered cities.

9

EGYPT

Thutmose III (XVIII Dynasty, 1490–1436) "...arrived at the city of Kadesh, overthrew it, cut down its groves, harvested its grains..." (Breasted, *Ancient Records* II, 465) Seti I (XIX Dynasty, 1303–1290) records at Karnak: "The town which his majesty built anew at the Wall of Hu-Ti..."; and in nearly the same breath tells of "...smiting the towns... destroying the settlements"; and in a famous victory hymn Merneptah (1223–1211) rejoices, "...their cities are made ashes, wasted, desolated; their seed is not..." (Breasted, *Ancient Records* III, 79, 141, 604).

ASSYRIA

Tukulti-Ninurta I (1244–1208) built Assur's city. Kar Tukulti Ninurta...

in the wastes of the flooded fields where
neither house nor dwelling existed.

Luckenbill, *Ancient Records* I, 167

and Adad-Nirari II (912–892) boasts:

The King, powerful in battle, who overthrows cities, who burnt the mountains of the land, am I.

Luckenbill, *Ancient Records* I, 359

Shalmaneser III (858–825) states with equal pride:

Arsashkun, the royal city of Arame of Urartu, I captured, I destroyed, I devastated, I burnt with fire...

Luckenbill, *Ancient Records* I, 619

and

at that time I rebuilt the walls of my city Assur from their foundations to their summits...

Luckenbill, *Ancient Records* I, 683

And in a similar vein, Sargon II (722–705) records his achievements:

With mighty battering rams I smashed the fortified walls and levelled them to the ground. The peoples and possessions I carried off; their cities I destroyed. I devastated, I burnt with fire... And at that time I built a city with the labor of the peoples of the lands which my hands had conquered... according to the command of God and the prompting of my heart, and I called it "Dur-Sharrukin."

Luckenbill, *Ancient Records* II, 6

ANATOLIA

In a Hittite chronicle we read about Mursilis I (1595):

then he marched to Halpa (Aleppo). He destroyed Halpa and brought the prisoners and the wealth of Halpa to Hattusas. Then he marched to Babylon and he destroyed Babylon. He beat the Hurrians and held the prisoners and the wealth of Babylon in Hattusas.

Schmökel, *Kulturgeschichte*, 344

And in another text,

> In the land of Hatti nobody before me built fortified cities. Thus I, Hantilis, put up fortified cities in the whole country. Also, the city of Hattusas have I, Hantilis, fortified.
>
> (Hantilis I, 1590–1560) Schmökel, *Kulturgeschichte*, 347

PALESTINE

The progress of the Israelites is marked by the capture of the main Canaanite cities, such as Jericho (Jos. 2:20–24) (13th century):

> The people went out into the city, every man straight before him, and they took the city. And they utterly destroyed all that was in the city, both man and woman, young and old, and ox and sheep and ass, with the edge of the sword... and they burnt the city with fire and all that was therein...

Building and rebuilding of cities could begin only with Solomon (961–922) after the consolidation of the Israelite conquest (I Kings 9:17–19):

> and Solomon built Gezer and Beth-horon, the nether, and Baalath and Tadmor in the wilderness, in the land; and all the cities of store that Solomon had, and cities for his chariots, and cities for his horsemen...

Representations of cities in the art of the ancient Near East are largely confined to the pictorial records of Egypt and Assyria. The reliefs, most in stone and a few in bronze, extol and commemorate the warlike exploits of the great kings. In one of the oldest of these representations, King Narmer (First Dynasty of Egypt) represented as a "Mighty Bull," attacks the fortified enclosure of a city (Fig. 2).

Most of our extant Egyptian reliefs picturing cities are related to campaigns of the XVIIIth and XIXth Dynasties. In them, cities are reduced to a few typical features—walls, gates, towers, windows, battlements—but essential characteristics of topography and geography are generally denoted. On a relief recording Sethos I's victory over the Canaanites near the border fortress of Sile, the town is virtually reduced to a symbol, a condensed image of a *Migdol* (Canaanite fort) (Fig. 3). The city of Ashkelon on a relief of Ramses II is abbreviated to a similar ideogram (Fig. 4). That such an ideogram or symbol can convey actual characteristics of a site is shown by comparing the fortified city of Kadesh on the Orontes, as depicted in a relief in Abu Simbel (Fig. 5), with a sketch plan of its actual emplacement (Fig. 6).

Assyrian reliefs are generally more detailed; they show more of the topographical setting, more "landmarks" denoting a particular site, and more architectural characteristics of the country, although the cities are also simplified to their most essential features. On the bronze gates of Shalmaneser III, for instance, the island character of Tyre (Fig. 7) is clearly indicated, and in the case of Parga (Fig. 8), a typical fortified Syrian river town is represented. The essential character of a Median city is brought out in a relief from the palace of Sargon II depicting the capture and burning of Kishesim (Fig. 9). In another of Sargon's reliefs, the Urartian town of Musasir (Fig. 10) with its temple of Bagbartu is well

11

characterized. Even more detailed are two reliefs from Assurbanipal's palace in Nineveh extolling his triumph over Elam, in which the cities of Der (Fig. 11) and Madaktu (Fig. 12) are represented. The symbolic nature of certain Assyrian city representations becomes evident from the city-models carried by city governors as tokens of submission, as depicted in a relief from Khorsabad (Fig. 13). The bronze fragments found at Toprakkale (Fig. 14) may have been part of such a city model.

The rim of a clay vessel found in Bogazköy (Fig. 15) gives us our only clue to the appearance of the superstructure of a Hittite city enclosure: A crenelated wall surmounted by a tower.

A few fragments of Mesopotamian clay tablets with city plans or maps have come to light. An Akkadian map of c. 2500 B.C., found at Nuzi (Fig. 16), locates three cities in a plain watered by a river and some canals, situated between two mountain ranges. An accurate scale map of Nippur (Fig. 17) was drawn in c. 1500 B.C., featuring walls, city gates, rivers and canals, and important landmarks such as temples, shrines and a "central park." Finally, part of a plan of Babylon from the Chaldean period shows a section of the "New City," with a city gate and a canal (Fig. 18).

While the foregoing quotations and depictions highlight certain features of cities in the ancient Near East, the following chapters—based on the latest evidence—will give a more complete picture of these cities against the environmental background of their respective countries. We will also scrutinize the characteristic planning practices of each region.

12

MESOPOTAMIA

Geographically, Mesopotamia,* in the narrow sense of the name, comprises the land between the rivers Tigris and Euphrates; in a wider sense, it is the whole alluvial plain created by the two great rivers and their tributaries, the Khabur, the Lower and Upper Zab, the Diyala, and finally the Kerkhah and the Karun. This whole large river basin, the eastern horn of the "Fertile Crescent," which extends westward into the North Syrian Plain, forms a geographic unity framed by the mountain ranges and foothills of Armenia and Kurdistan to the north, the Amanus and Anti-Taurus in the northwest, the Zagros range to the east, and the plateau of the Syrian desert in the west.

Climatically, northern Mesopotamia differs from the south; summer temperatures are more moderate, and winter rains are mostly adequate for agriculture, while in the south irrigation is a necessity. Unlike the regular inundation of the Nile, the floods of the Tigris and Euphrates—both rising in the Armenian highlands—are violent and unpredictable. Irrigation, flood control and drainage, to wash out the salts deposited with the silt, could be maintained only by an elaborate communal organization. This guaranteed a life of abundance, however, made possible by the rich yield of the fertile alluvial soil.

A large surplus of agricultural products released part of the population to other diversified and specialized activities, eventually creating a stratified society. A great increase in population led to the multiplication of large communal centers of an urban character. In the middle of the Fourth Millennium B.C., the lower Euphrates-Tigris basin was dotted with a great number of prosperous walled cities surrounded by their irrigation systems, fields and villages (Fig. 19), and centered around the temple precinct of the patron god to whom city and land were thought to belong; they were organized as independent self-contained states.

These city-states were governed by an assembly of elders who delegated to one man, called "Ensi," the authority to rule. He acted as the god's steward in a kind of theocratic state, administering the temple estates on behalf of the city god and originally combining priestly with secular functions. In case of war he was given emergency powers as "Lugal" (great man); but the concentration of power in one hand ultimately led to abuses, territorial ambitions, and the establishment of a kingdom.

Today, most of the ancient cities are but mounds in the desert, far away from the great rivers which have changed their courses. The once navigable canals and irrigation channels are long silted up and mostly dry, although still recognizable. Originally all cities were situated along water courses that not only provided drinking water but also served as

*See maps A and B.

13

the main means of communication. Land roads for donkey caravans followed these waterways. Mesopotamia had to import everything the soil did not bring forth, and from the earliest times on timber, metals, and luxury goods had to be brought from afar—copper, for instance, from Anatolia and Cyprus; building timber for major constructions all the way from the Amanus and the Lebanon.

Although the ruin-mounds of a great number of the ancient cities of Mesopotamia have been explored, only comparatively small areas have been thoroughly excavated because of the large size of the cities, the great depth of accumulated occupational debris of centuries or sometimes millennia, and the expense of the excavation involved. Sometimes, as at Arbil, no excavation has been possible at all because of continued occupation, and often, as for instance in Babylon, the early occupational levels lie under the present water table. In many cases, however, the vicissitudes of a city with its history of destructions and rebuildings can can be disentangled layer by layer.

Areas of Urban Concentration

A glance at the map of ancient Mesopotamia shows that concentrations of cities occur in three areas: In lower Mesopotamia, within the wide loop of the Euphrates and the Tigris, and south of it, the land of ancient Sumer; in the region occupying the narrow waist between the two rivers and extending to the lower Diyala River basin, roughly conforming to ancient Akkad; and in the "Assyrian Heartland" extending from Assur northward to the "Assyrian Triangle," the region between the Tigris and the Upper Zab River.

CITIES OF ANCIENT MESOPOTAMIA

1. Sumer

Ur (Tell Muqaiyar) is up to the present the most extensively explored Sumerian city and may thus serve as a typical example (Fig. 20). At the time of its greatest political power as capital of the Neo-Sumerian Empire under Ur-Nammu (2112–2095 B.C.) the inner city of Ur occupied an irregularly shaped mound, trapezoidal in the north and ovoid in the south; it was surrounded by a huge glacis-like mud-brick rampart crowned by a burnt-brick wall. This rampart served as a kind of retaining wall for the mound which, by this time, had risen from its beginnings in Ubaid times (Fourth Millennium B.C.) to considerable height. The city stood strategically on a promontory between an arm of the Euphrates and a navigable canal and was provided with two harbors. Off the center of the city to the northwest, on a terrace which had its corners oriented to the cardinal points, stood the walled temenos of the tutelary deity Nannar, the moon god. With its offices, storerooms, and temple compounds, this temenos served as administrative center of the city; it was dominated by its ziggurat. The palace of the ruler lay outside the

14

temple enclosure. The temenos underwent many periods of construction, the last major one under Nebuchadnezzar (604–561 B.C.); it reached its greatest extent at that time, when the city had already lost all its political and economic importance and become mainly a religious center. The population of the walled city of Ur at its peak has been estimated at 34,000 people in an area of 89 hectares,* but "Greater Ur" with its suburbs, merchant quarters, and dependencies might have been a city of a quarter of a million people. At *Uruk* (Warka, the "Erech" of the Old Testament) (Fig. 21), the largest of the ancient Sumerian cities, which occupied within its walls an area of 502.2 hectares, the famous ramparts built in Early Dynastic times (Third Millennium B.C.) have been traced in their entirety. They consisted of a double wall, 9.5 km. long,+ reinforced by nearly a thousand semicircular bastions (Fig. 22). The center of the city was occupied by the Eanna, the temple complex of the goddess Inanna, which in the Uruk period (c. 3500–3000 B.C.) consisted of a group of splendid temples and other monumental buildings—later surmounted by Ur-Nammu's ziggurat (c. 2100 B.C.)—and the temple terrace of the Anu sanctuary. The city flourished mainly in the Uruk, Protoliterate and Early Dynastic periods (c. 3500–2300 B.C.), and although it survived until the third century A.D., this was due only to the fame of its ancient shrines.

Eridu (Abu Shahrein), according to legend the earliest city in history, owed its fame to the E-Apsu, the venerable sanctuary of Ea-Enki. Originally bordering the sea or a lagoon it prospered in the late Ubaid and Uruk periods (Fourth Millennium B.C.); but already at the time of the Third Dynasty of Ur (2112–2004 B.C.) the city had been largely abandoned due to desiccation of the countryside and was preserved only in a reduced area as a religious center.

Kisiga (Tell el Lahm), *Larsa* (Senkereh), *Shuruppak* (Fara), *Isin* (Bahriyat), *Kisurra* (Abu Hatab), *Adab* (Bismaya), *Umma* (Djokha) and *Lagash* (Tello) were major Sumerian cities which played at various times, from the Early Dynastic through the Neo-Sumerian period, leading roles in the cultural and political life of the country.

Nippur (Niffar) (Fig. 23), situated in the geographical center between Sumer and Akkad, was never a politically independent city-state. Yet as the seat of Enlil, head of the Sumerian pantheon, it was the religious and cultural center of the land and, with an area of 323 hectares, one of its largest cities. Although it lost importance in the Second Millennium B.C. because of the rise of Babylon, it was occupied until the tenth century A.D. The city at its zenith was divided by a branch of the Euphrates River into two equal parts: one to the east comprising the E-kur, the temple precinct of Enlil with its ziggurat, administrative quarters, archives, etc., and one to the west with residential and commercial quarters. Small mounds scattered around the walled city suggest the

*1 hectare = 2.47 acres.
+1 kilometer = .62 miles.

15

remnants of a large suburban district. The Nippur map (Fig. 17), already mentioned, conforms closely to the archaeological evidence.

2. Akkad

Sippar (Abu Habba), one of the legendary antediluvian cities and *Kish* (Tell Ahaimir), seat of the "First Dynasty after the Flood" according to the "Sumerian King List," owed their importance to their location at the narrow waist between the great rivers, which gave them control over the main routes of the country. This must have been also the case with *Agade*—a site not yet discovered—the capital of Sargon I (2334–2279 B.C.) of Akkad. (In this same region, at various times in history, Babylon, Seleucia, Ctesiphon and Baghdad became capital cities of large realms.)

Eshnunna (Tell Asmar) (Fig. 24), *Tutub* (Khafajah), and *Nerebtum* (Ishchali) were important urban centers in the fertile lower Diyala River valley, mainly from the Early Dynastic to the Old Babylonian period (3000–1600 B.C.).

3. Central and Northern Mesopotamia

Mari (Tell Hariri), the "Tenth Royal and Dynastic City after the Flood" was the only major city in the middle Euphrates region. It controlled the trade routes by land and river to northern Syria and Anatolia and across the desert via Damascus to Palestine and the Mediterranean coast.

Tepe Gawra, the "Great Mound," lies north of Nineveh in the hill country between the Tigris and the Upper Zab. Twenty distinct strata of occupation have been partially excavated. No evidence of Assyrian or later times has been found. The first urban settlement belongs to the Uruk period (Level XIA, 3500–3200 B.C.) (Fig. 25). A strongly fortified, citadel-like round building occupies the center of the town in a semi-isolated position, surrounded by dense clusters of small, mostly attached houses separated by irregular lanes. There is no peripheral enclosure, but the buildings arranged in a jagged outline along the edge of the mound seem to have been part of a fortification system reinforced by watchtowers. The last important urban level (VI) (Fig. 26) belongs to Early Dynastic times, about 3000 B.C. Very compact agglomerations of buildings are arranged around a large, roughly rectangular square, from which narrow streets radiate. There is no town wall—again the fortress-like buildings around the periphery are part of the defense system.

Nuzi (Yorgan Tepe) (Fig. 27) lies in a well-watered plain off the foothills of the Kurdish Mountains. A Sargonid city, Ga-Sur, seems to have occupied the site toward the end of the Third Millennium B.C. The main stratum (II) shows it to have been a provincial Hurrian town in the Second Millennium B.C. The center of the roughly rectangular city (200 by 220 m.) * with a built-up area of about 4.4 hectares, is dominated by a large palace and a temple complex northwest of it. Except for another palace-like structure in the northern corner, the rest of the city

*1 meter = 39.37 inches.

is occupied by rather well-planned residential and commercial districts with mainly straight streets and square buildings. The city is oriented with its corners toward the cardinal points.

4. *Assyria*

Situated on a high bluff between the Tigris and a navigable river-arm, *Assur* (Qal'at Sherqat) (Fig. 28), first capital of the independent state of Assyria and residence city of the national god Assur, was a natural fortress dominating the trade routes along the upper Tigris. The original city with its palaces, temples and temple towers occupied the high ground to the north overlooking the Tigris arm and was exposed directly to the cool northwest wind. To the south lay the inner city with tightly built-up residential quarters. In the fifteenth century B.C. a "New City" was added in the southeast along the Tigris, the city wall extended, and a moat dug to make Assur a virtual island.

Kalhu (Nimrud, the "Calah" of the Bible), second capital of Assyria, was rebuilt by Assurnasirpal II (883–859 B.C.) on a grand scale (Fig. 29). Laid out in a vast rectangle, it was surrounded by a mud-brick rampart which enclosed an area of nearly 360 hectares. Along the Tigris, where probably the original town had stood, rose the fortified inner city (Fig. 30), planned as a citadel mainly devoted to palaces, temples, administration buildings and a small residential quarter for high government officials. The majority of the population, however, must have lived in the outer city in simple mud-brick houses and even tents. Large areas within the outer enclosure were probably taken up by fields, open spaces for flocks in case of war, parks and zoological gardens.

Two mounds on the left bank of the Tigris, one very large, Kuyunjik and a smaller one, Nebi Yunus, together with the remnants of the encircling ramparts, represent today the remains of *Nineveh* (Fig. 31). Kuyunjik seems to have been the site of the early city, of which we have evidence of occupational levels from the Fifth Millennium B.C. on. Metropolitan Nineveh, covering an area of 728.7 hectares with a probable population of over 170,000, was the creation of Sennacherib (704–681 B.C.). The city as planned by this monarch had the shape of an elongated triangle with the east side slightly convex and a truncated apex in the south. It was surrounded by an inner wall with fifteen gates. A huge outer wall, undoubtedly intended to encircle the city up to the Tigris was finished only in the east. A stream which endangered the inner city was diverted by Sennacherib to outside the city wall. Within the city the king had a great park laid out with all kinds of exotic plants and trees, a game reserve, and privately and publicly owned gardens and orchards. He also built a "kingsway," a triumphal road which was not to be encroached upon under penalty of death. To safeguard the water supply of the metropolis he dammed up the Khoser River, built a reservoir, and brought water through an aqueduct over a distance of 16 km. No residential quarters have been excavated to date.

Dur Sharrukin (Khorsabad) (Fig. 32), the short-lived and never finished new capital of Sargon II (721–705 B.C.), was built, as was Assurnasirpal's Kalhu and Sennacherib's Nineveh, with the slave labor resulting from military conquests. The city, square, with an area of 300 hectares, was surrounded by a strong wall with square towers. Seven irregularly spaced gates provided access. The fortified citadel was unexplainably placed off center against the northwestern city wall. The temenos with its temples, ziggurat, and palace was supported by a high platform, which rose inside the citadel and protruded on a bastion beyond the city enclosure. Access to citadel and temenos was possible only from the city. A fortress straddling the city wall was constructed off its southern corner. Practically no traces of built-up areas or streets have been found within the city.

5. *Babylonia*

The early city of *Babylon* lay on the left bank of the central arm of the old Euphrates, controlling the southern end of the "Mesopotamian Neck" and thus the trade routes from the Persian Gulf to the Mediterranean. Time and again it was ruthlessly destroyed by foreign invaders, most thoroughly by Sennacherib; it was as often rebuilt and its temples restored because of its importance as a religious center. The city as excavated is mainly the creation of Nebuchadnezzar II (604–561 B.C.). It has all the appearance of a planned city (Fig. 33). A rectangle with an area of 404.8 hectares, oriented with its corners toward the cardinal points, was surrounded by a double fortification wall reinforced by strong towers and a moat. A system of major streets led to the eight gates. The enormous holy precinct of Esagila, the temple of Marduk, main sanctuary of Babylon, and the Etemenanki, "The Foundation of Heaven and Earth" or "Tower of Babel", occupied the center of the city east of the Euphrates that separated the Old City from the "New City" (Fig. 34).

On a high platform just within the northern city ramparts, fortified by its own enclosure and with its own gateway, rose the Southern (main) Citadel (Fig. 35), a huge complex of administration and garrison buildings, palaces, throne room, and famous "Hanging Gardens"—all arranged around five enormous courtyards. Toward the Euphrates, Babylon was guarded by a formidable fortress. Nebuchadnezzar had the citadel further extended outside the city walls by the construction of a "Central" and a "Northern" citadel, the former housing his famous "museum" of the spoils of war. Parallel to the river, passing to the east of the Esagila and the citadel, led the monumental "Processional Way," leaving the city in the north through the Ishtar Gate toward the New Year's Festival house. An outer wall, south and east of the built-up city, also enclosing the summer palace on the mound Babil in the north, was constructed by Nebuchadnezzar as an additional bulwark. It extended the city's periphery to 18 km. without adding much to its population, as the enclosed area was intended mainly as a refuge from the unprotected countryside. A belt of suburbs with gardens and canals ringed the Greater City of Babylon, which might have numbered more than half a million inhabitants.

Borsippa (Birs Nimrud) also owes its final shape to Nebuchadnezzar II. It was planned as a regular rectangle with its corners oriented to the cardinal points and surrounded by a double wall and moat (Fig. 36). The main streets crossed each other at right angles. From the large temple compound of the patron god Nabu, called Ezida, a "Processional Way" led to the Borsippa Canal which linked the city with Babylon. To the northwest, exposed to the cool breezes of a lake, lay the palace and a well-to-do patricians' quarter. Numerous suburbs surrounded the city.

PLANNING

The following discussion will show that the people of Mesopotamia were as conservative in their approach to planning as they were in the architectural treatment of the plans and elevations of their individual buildings.

1. *Monumental Building Groups*

The first known complex of monumental buildings dates from about the middle of the Fourth Millennium B.C.—the end of the Ubaid period. In Stratum XIII of Tepe Gawra (Fig. 37) we see three temples around a large court, with some minor buildings to the northwest forming a kind of acropolis. According to the excavators, the eastern shrine must be regarded as the first unit built and the northern temple as the second. The plan shows that there has been great concern for balance and symmetry in the layout of the single buildings and their facades, but there is little regard for the alignment of the temples or their relationship to one another, although the northern temple might have been planned directly opposite the projecting wing of the eastern shrine. It will be seen that this concern for symmetry, axes, and balance within the individual unit, but disregard of an over-all compositional principle, remains typical for Mesopotamian planning throughout its history. Level VIIIC (Fig. 38) and VIIIA (Fig. 39) (3100–2900 B.C.) of Tepe Gawra are examples of the same tendency during the following Protoliterate period. The temples of the archaic levels IVA (Fig. 40) and IVB-V (Fig. 41) (3300–3100 B.C.) in the Eanna temenos of the city of Uruk show again a sense of perfection and harmony with regard to the single buildings, but an indifferent juxtaposition within the holy precinct.

When a single temple is put on a platform or on a high terrace as the painted shrine at *Uqair* (Fig. 42) and the "White Temple" of Anu at Uruk (Fig. 43) at the beginning of the succeeding Jemdet Nasr period (3100–2900 B.C.), its relationship to the irregular supporting structure is haphazard and of no concern, provided that the religious concept of elevation or the idea of the sacred mountain has been realized.

Similar observations can be made with regard to the famous Temple Oval at Khafajah (Fig. 44) in the Early Dynastic period that follows. Considerations of straight or broken axes or symmetry do not extend to the planning of the whole complex.

This peculiar attitude of the Mesopotamian builders in planning is also revealed in their secular building. Their concern for formal planning, symmetry and axial approach is never consistently carried through but is only applied to parts of the building. After the general shape has been determined—according to expediency rather than any recognizable principle, like the topographical features of the site or the proximity of existing structures—narrow rectangular rooms are arranged around large courtyards as prime planning elements in an irregular functional pattern. The earliest preserved palace from the Early Dynastic period—at Kish (Fig. 45)—is a good example of the internal planning of such a structure and also of the relationship of the palace itself (I) to the gate building to the east (II) and the later palace (III) to the south. The Akkadian palace at Tell Asmar (A) (Fig. 24) shows the aforementioned characteristics even better.

In the Neo-Sumerian period, Mesopotamian monumental "planning" reaches its classic form, hardly to change any more. What might be called "the casemate system" of elongated narrow rooms in single or multiple rows around courtyards becomes the rule in the planning of both palaces and temples. Multiple gateways are used in this period in Mesopotamia long before they appear elsewhere. Under Ur Nammu (2112–2095 B.C.) the multistage ziggurat becomes a dominant feature of the temenos and the city, but its relationship to terrace court and forecourt, if we look at the example of the sacred precinct of Ur (Fig. 46), shows the same peculiarities already mentioned. New buildings are added by juxtaposition without any basic change in concept from the time of the Third Dynasty of Ur to the Chaldean Dynasty. The palace of the rulers of Eshnunna (D), the southern building (F) in the same city (Fig. 24), or the palace of Mari (Fig. 47), offers no advance in the planning of a monumental complex, except for sheer size. At Eshnunna (Fig. 24) the grouping of the Gimilsin Temple (E), the palace of the rulers (D), and the "South building" (F) of the Isin-Larsa period, the agglomeration of temples and palaces in Assur around the "temple square" (Fig. 28), the temenos complex near the ziggurat at Mari (Fig. 48), or the jumble of temples and palaces on the mound of Kuyunjik in Nineveh (Fig. 49) remind one very much of the beginning of monumental architecture at Tepe Gawra and Uruk. But nowhere do we get a clearer picture of this unconcern for organic planning than in the newly created citadels of Kalhu (Fig. 30) and Dur Sharrukin (Fig. 50). Here no existing buildings, no street layout, no adherence to a spot hallowed by tradition was interfering with the layout, location, and relationship of the new edifices. The odd angles of Nabu Temple, "Burnt Palace" and the governor's palace in Nimrud and the particularly awkward, unwarranted

20

layout of Nabu Temple, residences, and government buildings in Khorsabad make it clear that if there was any concept of planning it was restricted to individual building units or perhaps only to the elements of a building. This basic approach did not change either in the Neo-Babylonian period, as a glance at the Southern Citadel of Babylon (Fig. 35) or the temple precincts of Babylon (Fig. 33) or Borsippa (Fig. 51) show.

One principle generally adhered to throughout history was, however, that of orientation, although there are exceptions: Most buildings and cities face the northwest whence comes the most pleasant wind (called in literary sources "the favorable wind"). It is therefore not surprising that whenever possible the best dwellings, palaces, and citadels lay on the northwest side.

2. *Residential Quarters and Housing*

It will be seen that in the layout of residential quarters and the construction of housing districts there was no difference of principle between "grown" cities and "planned" cities. There was little prior planning at all except for some "zoning" for residential districts in newly created cities.

The city pattern develops from the house unit outward. The nucleus is a central court or living room around which the secondary rooms are grouped rather artlessly according to requirements and available space. Initially, there are open spaces around the irregularly located housing units which are generally oriented toward the prevailing breeze, and tracks rather than roads follow the established pattern of trails, trodden by flock, donkeys, and man to the fields and neighboring communities. With the growth of the population behind the fortified enclosure, the open spaces disappear, the irregular interstices between the single houses are filled by an agglomeration of other buildings, the thoroughfares are reduced to a minimum, and only narrow lanes and dead-end alleys are left to provide access to most houses. Rounded corners often ease the confined flow of traffic. Nowhere is any room left for gardens or green areas.

This process of "urban growth" is clearly evident in Level XIA (Fig. 25) at Tepe Gawra (c. 3300 B.C.) from the Uruk period. In Level VIIIA (Fig. 39) (c. 2900 B.C.) it can be observed how private houses start encroaching on the temple precinct and finally in Level VI (Fig. 26) of the beginning of the Third Millennium B.C. we can follow the formation of clusters of houses with access lanes and narrow passages. Some of the streets are paved and provided with drainage. Remnants of rather regularly laid-out house units with drains emptying out into a thoroughfare in Kish (Fig. 52) from the Pre-Sargonid period and remains of the residential quarter east of the Ishtar Temple in Mari (Fig. 53) are illustrative of the above-mentioned characteristics of city development. The growth from house nuclei is easily recognizable in Tell Asmar (C) (Fig. 24) and Khafajah (Fig. 54). The often-publicized residential areas of

Ur from the Larsa period, one, a seemingly well-to-do quarter with good-sized "townhouses" (Fig. 55), often of two stories, the other very congested by small dwellings interspersed with shops and workshops and small shrines (Fig. 56); these show no further advance in "planning."

The private houses erected in the citadel compound of Kalhu (Fig. 30) for especially privileged and important citizens and officials are still not laid out according to any regular plan, and the late Assyrian residential quarter over the ruins of Tukulti-Ninurta I's palace-terrace in Assur (Fig. 57) could as well hail from the Third Millennium B.C.

Much has been made of the "planned" Merkes quarter of Chaldean Babylon (Fig. 58). The apparent difference is only a matter of scale, not of inherent principle. As in the "Larsa" houses of Ur, large houses built around a central court lead to a quasi-rectilinear layout. It can be easily recognized that again the city pattern develops from the single nucleus, although of course major arteries of traffic are maintained in as straight an alignment as possible.

There are two interesting examples of what appear to be a "planned city" and a "planned city quarter": The walled quarter in Khafajah northeast of the Temple Oval (Fig. 59) from the Early Dynastic period, certainly built for a special purpose, is laid out in tightly packed rectangular blocks; but in studying the street pattern and the individual housing units, it becomes apparent that the only underlying principle is economy of space, with no particular concept of planning.

Shaduppum (Tell Abu-Harmal) (Fig. 60) has all the appearance of a newly created city, probably built as a fortified administration center during the Isin-Larsa period (2025–1763 B.C.). But if there was any concept of a geometrical plan it was not carried through. A great effort is made to achieve an even rhythm in the spacing of the towers, buttresses and panels of the enclosing wall, but there is no concern for regularity of the over-all shape. The only city gate is symmetrically designed, but its location is awkward. The main artery leading from it and also the side streets are not straight but broken and encroached upon by projecting buildings.

It becomes again evident that the Mesopotamian architect or builder was not concerned with an over-all composition or with comprehensive pre-planning but only with individual edifices. The latter were placed according to their importance, function, or convenience, where there was desirable open ground. Additional buildings, always planned from the inside out, were then juxtaposed or fitted into the available space, leaving necessary thoroughfares and access lanes free for traffic.

EGYPT

Ancient Egypt's* cultural development was to a large extent predestined by its unique geographic and climatic conditions. Upper Egypt, from its natural southern border below the first cataract of the Nile north to *On* (Heliopolis) where the mountains recede and the river originally divided into several arms, was confined to a deep and narrow canyon-like valley, 650 km. long and 16 to 50 km. wide, which the Nile has cut into the limestone plateau. The cultivable strip of fertile black soil deposited by the river up to a depth of 10 m. is seldom more than 10 km. in width. Lower Egypt comprised the "Delta," as the Greeks called the triangle of rich alluvial deposits, not more than 150 km. from its apex to its base at the Mediterranean Sea, which measures about 200 km.

On both sides "Tomeri" (the "Two Lands of Egypt") was protected and effectively isolated by vast deserts which left open to intrusion and also expansion, both cultural and military, only the coastal region in the north and the Nile valley itself in the south.

Without the Nile, Egypt, a country with eternally sunny skies and therefore without rain except in the northern Delta, would have been a desert wasteland. Herodotus has aptly called Egypt a "gift of the river." The Nile was the source and sustaining force of its life. It provided for its livelihood and was also its great artery of communication. The annual inundations of the river caused by the melting of the snows and heavy spring rains in the Abyssinian highlands were predictable and reliable; they not only established a firm rhythm of seasonal occupations for the population but also led to the concept of an established cosmic order that safeguarded eternal renewal and promised permanence of life after death—ideas which found ultimate expression in the monumental mortuary art and architecture of ancient Egypt.

The fact that Egyptians gave more importance to their afterlife than to their life on earth led to their choice of stone for funerary monuments, while dwellings, residences and even palaces, being temporary structures, were built with cheaper, non-enduring materials like mud-brick and wood. No wonder then that tomb structures and, of course, temples as permanent abodes of gods have largely survived, while secular buildings, towns, and cities have been preserved only by exceptionally good fortune. In addition, the silt deposited by the river for centuries in the Delta and in the Nile Valley has covered many ancient sites, while city quarters lying on higher ground, still extant a century ago—as for instance at Memphis and El Kab—have vanished owing to the activity of "Sebakhin," diggers of decayed brick valued as fertilizer.

On the obverse side of the Narmer palette (Fig. 2), as we have already seen, the king, represented by a mightly bull, destroys a city symbolized

*See maps A and C.

by a bastioned oval rampart with sanctuary and houses, and on another late Predynastic palette (Fig. 61), a number of stongly fortified cities with square enclosures are depicted along with symbols of houses and emblems of occupants and attackers.

These early representations of plans of fortified cities are unique for Egypt. There are no subsequent ones. The city as such is never shown in the rich repertory of Egyptian pictorial art, although what appear to be single townhouses are depicted in scenes of everyday life: fortified cities of Palestine and Syria are portrayed on the campaign reliefs of the warlike kings of the XIX Dynasty, as we have seen, but only as a record of their military conquest and destruction.

There can be no doubt that cities existed in ancient Egypt as early as Predynastic times. The character of Egyptian cities varies, however, according to their period. Before the first unified monarchy, and during times of breakdown of central power, the city appears as an autonomous organism, sometimes under a local overlord, distinct from the feudal organization of the countryside. In times of strongly centralized government the cities have no special rights or jurisdiction and become mere administrative or cult centers with a population performing diversified duties of service, trade, and crafts. The strongly autonomous civic organization based on an enormous communal effort, which led to the growth of the Sumerian cities, never developed in Egypt. No comparative communal enterprise was required, and the early unification of the country under one indisputable central authority left little room for development of autonomous city-states.

In the Protohistoric period the Delta seems to have comprised a great number of cities organized with their surrounding land as small city-states, each under its king, while the south was divided into feudal principalities of rather rural character with fortified towns as centers. A loose federation of the northern city-states and of the southern principalities preceded the ultimate unification of the "Two Lands."

Two ancient hieroglyphs shed some light on the early regional organization of the country. The sign for "spat" (Fig. 62), territorial division or district, called by the Greeks "nome," is a rectangle divided by intersecting lines into squares, originally the criss-crossing of dikes. The sign "nut" (Fig. 63), town, is a circular enclosure around a road crossing or around some blocks of buildings. Each nome comprised a territory and its capital which was originally only a fortified place at a "crossing" to which the population could retire for safety, with a shrine of the patron deity, a mansion for the nomarch (ruler of the nome) or royal administrator, and a market for the exchange of products. The later ensigns designating these nomes carry in their totemistic symbols the memory of their origin in a clan-organization of prehistoric times. Other towns were often founded by royal decree as urban centers for the growing population on newly reclaimed agricultural land extending into the adjacent desert.

24

One type of "city" is a purely ancient Egyptian phenomenon: The so-called pyramid cities, prevalent during the Old and Middle Kingdom, were created by royal charter to house the workmen and masons constructing the pyramids and—after their completion—the priests performing the royal funerary services, as well as tenant farmers and laborers who worked the land set aside for the purpose of producing revenue for the continued maintenance of the monument and its ritual duties. The citizens of these towns were exempted by royal decree from any other compulsory labor or taxes.

It should also be mentioned here that there was no single permanent capital in ancient Egypt. Kings of the various dynasties built new capital cities in locations which seemed strategically and politically desirable at the time—as at Memphis, Ith-Towe, Avaris, Pi-Ramesse and Bubastis—or chose existing cities in which they held controlling power as their capital, as Heracleopolis, Thebes, Tanis and Sais.

CITIES OF ANCIENT EGYPT

1. *The Delta*

The cities of the Delta, such as *Wazet, Sais, Busiris, Athribis, Mendes, Bubastis* and *Tanis* developed nearby navigable canals or arms of the Nile, which provided their only access and means of communication. All were river ports and depended heavily on trade both within the country and overseas (mainly with the Levant) for their subsistence. Only few remains have been found to date.

Wazet (Buto) was the Predynastic capital of Lower Egypt, consisting actually of two separate cities: Dep, the sacred city of Wazet, the cobra goddess, later to become the emblematic deity of Lower Egypt, and Pe, the city of Horus and royal residence.

Avaris, the capital of the Asiatic Hyksos during their rule over Northern Egypt (c. 1730–1580 B.C.) controlled the easternmost Tanitic branch of the Nile and one of the main routes into Egypt. In this strategic location Ramses II (1290–1224 B.C.) built his new residence city *Pi-Ramesse*, resplendent with shrines, royal palaces, and gardens beautified by statuary pilfered from temples built under earlier dynasties in the Fayum and Memphis. This city, under the name *Tanis*, became the main harbor for the Levant trade.

The fortress towns of *Sile* and *Pi-Tum* guarded the chief approaches into the Delta from the east.

Both *On* (Heliopolis), with its temple of the sun god, one of the most important religious centers, and *Memphis*, the capital of Egypt during the time of the Old Kingdom (2780–2258 B.C.), second largest city and northern capital at the time of the "Empire" and great metropolis of the late periods, were situated near the apex of the Delta. Ancient Memphis, a great port city, agricultural, trading, administrative and religious center, included besides the residential quarters for its cosmopolitan population a great number of temples and palaces, industrial and commercial districts with wharves, warehouses, workshops, and business establishments, as well as large open areas with lakes and parks; its actual extent is not known. Only a few ruins, from the time of Ramses II, remain (Fig. 64). A clue to the size of "Greater Memphis" might be derived from the sprawling necropolises of the III to the VI "Memphite" Dynasties to the west, which were probably not far from their respective residences that clustered around the religious and administrative capital. The origin of the city is ascribed to Menes (c. 3200 B.C.) who founded for the centralized control of his newly united monarchy the royal city and citadel of "White Wall" at the "Balance of the Two Lands" at the tip of the Delta—on a site widened by the diversion of the Nile toward the east. Pepi I's pyramid city of Men-Nefer (VI Dynasty) gave the city, in its Greek transliteration, the name "Memphis."

2. *Middle Egypt and the Fayum*

Ith-Towe, the "Captor of the Two Lands," was founded by Amenemhet I, first king of the XII Dynasty (1991–1962 B.C.) as his new capital to control both northern and southern Egypt. The city, not yet discovered, must have been situated at the border of the Fayum district, where Amenemhet's pyramid has been found. Succeeding rulers of the XII Dynasty undertook vast reclamation and irrigation projects in the Fayum, the easternmost oasis of the Libyan Desert, by controlling the inflow of the Nile arm Bahr Yusuf into Lake Qarun (the Greek Lake Moeris) and by using the lake as storage reservoir. New towns sprang up in this province (until Roman times one of the most flourishing of Egypt), as for instance *Shedet*, called by the Greeks "Crocodilopolis."

The pyramid city of Sesostris II (1897–1879 B.C.) near his pyramid at Illahun, *Hotep Sesostris*, now called Kahun (Fig. 65), is preserved in its greater part. Within a rectangular mud-brick enclosure the city was constructed according to a preconceived plan providing maximal occupancy on a minimal area and zoned according to its different types of buildings. A wall separated the western quarter for workers and craftsmen from the rest of the town occupied in the north by a group of very large townhouses for government officials, and to the south by residential quarters, probably for professional workmen of a higher standing, and stores. The houses, grouped according to standard types, were arranged in large blocks of single or double row houses accessible by side streets branching off at right angles from a main artery. One gate in the east leading into the main street has been preserved; others must have permitted entry from the south. A walled "acropolis" with the king's residential palace on a high platform next to the northern wall, entered from a large open square protected by a guardhouse, dominated the northern part of the city, while a temple on high ground surrounded on three sides by an enormous wall commanded its southern part. Apparently no gardens or parks could be afforded within the tightly built-up space. The city probably existed for less than a century.

In the comparatively wide fertile strip of land between the Nile and the Bahr Yusuf a number of urban centers became strongholds of powerful feudal lords. *Nen Nesu* (Heracleopolis), *Oxyrynchus*, *Shmunu* (Hermopolis) and *Asyut* (Lycopolis) gained prominence mainly during periods of weakness of the central government. On the opposite bank of the Nile, southeast of Shmunu, lie the ruins of *El Amarna* (Fig. 66). Here, in a wide sandy bay surrounded by the mountain fringes of the Eastern Desert, remote from the inimical influence of the Theban priesthood of Amun, Amenhotep IV, (Akhenaten) (1364–1347 B.C.), had built his new residence city Akhetaten ("Horizon of Aten"), dedicated to the one and only god Aten. An artificial creation of short duration, atypical for ancient Egypt, it is today besides the much smaller Kahun the only settlement preserved in its organic whole. Unlike most Egyptian cities it had no walls because the river and cliffs provided adequate protection. No over-all guiding principle in the layout of the city can be recognized. The availability of water—in the form of wells or channels from the river—confined it to a narrow strip along the low-lying margin of cultivated land bordering the Nile. The major structural complexes— the great temple of Aten and the central palace with their dependencies —were built along the north-south artery at the edge of the cultivation, the main residential quarters along two parallel streets to the southeast.

3. *Upper Egypt*

This, capital of the Thinite nome and probable native city and capital of the kings of the first two dynasties of the unified monarchy (c. 3200–2870 B.C.) has not yet been located. It must have been situated to the north of *Abydos* where tombs of the early kings, their families, and retainers have been found (cf. Figs. 72, 73), as well as the fortified enclosures of what are thought to have been the Upper Egyptian residences of two kings of the II Dynasty. The main caravan route to the oasis of El Kharga in the Libyan Desert to the west, which started near Abydos, gave the city commercial importance.

Coptos, lying east of the great bend which brings the Nile closest to the Red Sea, was the point of departure and arrival for the caravans across the desert, through the valley of Rohanu (Hammamat), to and from the coastal ports that were engaged in lucrative trade with the lands of Punt east and west of the South Arabian Sea. It was also the center of one of the most important gold mining regions of ancient Egypt and was the city closest to the famous quarries of the Hammamat which had been exploited since the earliest times.

After reaching *Hermonthis*, another ancient nome capital, the Nile turns out of its hitherto northwesterly direction sharply to the northeast and the cliffs on the east bank open up into a wide fertile plain—an ideal location for a large city. Today only a gigantic stone skeleton remains of the living organism of the great city of *Thebes* (Fig. 67), "the Mistress of Every City," capital of the Egyptian Empire (XVIII-XX Dynasties). This comprises the ruins of the enormous temple compounds of Luxor and Karnak on the eastern bank of the river and the string of great mortuary temples beneath the towering cliffs of the Western Desert, where the Pharaohs of the New Kingdom dug their rock tombs, to the west. Of the actual city of Thebes nothing remains. The major residential quarters probably lay on the west side of the Nile between the river bank and the mortuary temples and the palace and the lake of Amenhotep III at the fringe of the desert. The eastern city comprised two separate quarters, the northern "Opet of Amun" around the temple complex of Karnak (Fig. 68) and the "Southern Opet" around the temple of Luxor, each enclosed by its own mud-brick wall and linked with one another by an avenue of sphinxes (the western one). As the temples grew, the residential and commercial quarters within the enclosures became more and more congested, spilling over into the open country-side and developing into extended suburbs around the official buildings and palaces set in luxurious gardens and parks along the avenue of sphinxes and along the riverbank. There is no evidence that the sprawling metropolis was fortified by a wall. The famous remark of Herodotus about the "hundred gates of Thebes" must have referred to the many pylons of the temple complexes and not to city gates.

Nekheb (El Kab), the Predynastic capital of the Southern Kingdom before the conquest of Lower Egypt, occupied an easily defensible position on the eastern bank of the Nile not far north of the original border with Nubia (Figs. 70, 71). It seems that the early importance and power of the city in a region where arable land was scarce, derived from control of the river traffic and exploitation of natron and particularly gold and silver mines in the mountains to the east. The tutelary deity of the city, the vulture goddess Nekhbet, became one of the emblematic symbols of Upper Egypt. Opposite Nekheb across the river lay the sister city of *Nekhen*, the holy city of Horus (Greek "Hierakonpolis") and res-idence of the rulers of the Predynastic Southern Kingdom whose white crown later symbolized the kingship over Upper Egypt (Fig. 69). As Dep, sacred city of the cobra goddess Wazet, together with Pe, royal city of Horus, formed Wazet (Buto) the ancient capital of the north, so Nekhen probably functioned as part of the capital city of the south. The ancient enclosure walls of both towns, traceable to the Early Dynastic period, have been preserved. At Nekhen (Fig. 69) the wall of crude brick is trapezoidal in shape. A large temenos with a temple occupies the southern quarter of the town, built around an ancient oval shrine. The area between temenos and town enclosure seems to have been densely built up. The old town of Nekheb (Fig. 70) was surrounded by a double oval wall of crude brick, but only the northeastern quadrant is extant; the rest of the town has been washed away by the river. At a time when the slowly rising Nile had threatened the old town, a grandiose scheme for a new city was initiated and an enormous rectangular mud-brick wall (Fig. 71), 12 m. thick and 11 m. high with five gates, three ramps, and a quay actually built. Yet while the old town continued to flourish through the XXX Dynasty (4th cent. B.C.) the new city area was never occupied.

PLANNING IN ANCIENT EGYPT

The remains of most ancient Egyptian cities are too sparse and isolated to allow definitive judgments about their planning, but some conclusions can be drawn from the combination of available archaeological evidence and analogies to the much better preserved monumental ruins of mortuary and sacred architecture in stone.

The few remnants of Early Dynastic houses within the enclosure of Nekhen (Fig. 69) are not sufficient to get an idea about the layout of the town. They imply mostly rectangular rooms, rather uniform orientation, and growth probably by agglomeration. To follow the progress of Egyptian planning under the first dynasties we have to look at tomb structures, of which quite a number have been excavated. The tomb of King Zer (Fig. 72), third king of the First Dynasty at Abydos (c. 3150 B.C.), shows a rather awkward relationship of his tomb structure to the surrounding rows of subsidiary graves of retainers, as well as an irregular layout of the magazines around the tomb chamber on the inside. King Ka'a's tomb at Abydos (Fig. 73), toward the end of the dynasty (c. 3000 B.C.), shows a more integrated compact composition of the elements. A similar and parallel development can be traced at Saqqara, where planning was more advanced. There, tomb 3505 (Fig. 74), traceable to King Ka'a's reign, features a carefully conceived arrangement with systematic handling of the design components. Within the incredibly short span of three hundred years, complete mastery was achieved in Imhotep's great funerary complex for King Zoser (c. 2700 B.C.) at Saqqara (Fig. 75). It demonstrates planning on the grandest scale—city planning for a mortuary city. Here the Egyptian genius for playing off heavy masses of masonry against vast open spaces, for the articulation of building elements, for balance or symmetry of solids and voids, and for the sophisticated use of straight and broken axes, has found full expression. While building programs and styles might vary, the principles of design and planning established at Saqqara at the beginning of the III Dynasty for monumental tomb complexes hardly changed during the rest of Egyptian history.

The functional program of the Pyramid-and-Valley Temple (Fig. 76) of Chefren of the IV Dynasty might differ from that of the pyramid complex of Sahure (Fig. 77) of the V Dynasty, or from that of the mortuary temple of Mentuhotep II (Fig. 78) of the XI Dynasty or the pyramid temple of Sesostris I (Fig. 79) of the XII Dynasty, and indeed the elements of the composition could be of a different nature, but the philosophy of planning is the same. There is a consistent predilection for axial balance and symmetry, for crystal-clear disposition of components and for a climactic or anti-climactic sequence of building masses or voids.

All funerary monuments mentioned so far were ordered by a king and planned and built for him. We now have to ask whether the same principles of planning applied to other types of construction as well. The IV Dynasty cemetery at Giza (Fig. 80) provides a partial answer. East and west of the great pyramid of Cheops we can discern the orderly, orthogonally laid-out rows of large mastabas (tomb structures) planned and built by order of the king for the members of his family and court. Around them cluster in haphazard fashion the later tombs, built individually by permission rather than by royal fiat. It will be seen that this coexistence of planning and uncontrolled growth in a funerary city is not an isolated case but symptomatic of the prevalent conditions in the cities of ancient Egypt.

While we lack, as already stated, any knowledge of a layout or even of a partial plan for any town or city of the Old Kingdom, a "Pyramid City" from the end of the IV or beginning of the V Dynasty has fortunately been preserved, nearly in its entirety, at Giza (Fig. 81). This "city," a part of the pyramid complex of Queen Khent-Kawes and enclosed within its wall, was obviously designed and built in its entirety to house the priests and servants of the pyramid. North of a main street and causeway lies a quarter consisting of attached and nearly identical row houses with a service alley along their rear. A cross street leads from a northern gate through an underpass under the causeway to a quarter of large mansions separated from each other by streets. The layout is strictly orthogonal, the orientation north-south.

The largest pyramid city known to date is *Hotep Sesostris* (Fig. 65) at Kahun at the edge of the Fayum, built, as we have seen, by Sesostris II during the Middle Kingdom. Here the principles of planning observed in the pyramid city of Queen Khent-Kawes are applied on a larger scale. Buildings have been further standardized according to types, and grouped within special pre-established zones.

More light is shed on secular planning by a string of fortress towns (Fig. 82) constructed by powerful kings of the XII Dynasty along the "Batn el Hagar," or "Belly of Stone" as the rocky rapids of the Second Cataract were called, in order to control traffic between Upper and Lower Nubia, to provide safe trading posts with the South, and to protect the border. Within formidable enclosure walls (Fig. 83), their shape adapted to the topographical conditions of the site and nearly all fortified by towers, the town quarters were laid out for maximal efficiency and control in orthogonally arranged blocks with each type of building standardized according to its function. A military ring road inside the ramparts connects water and land gates which feed in most cases directly into one of the major arterial roads of the town, from which secondary streets branch off.

A larger fortress town in Upper Nubia below the Third Cataract was probably built under Akhenaten on the site of an earlier XVIII Dynasty settlement with later additions and alterations made by Sethos I. At *Sesebi* (Fig. 89) a pre-planned over-all layout is clearly lacking. The planning is restricted to the individual building complexes themselves —temples, magazines, and residential quarter—which were juxtaposed without any coherent organization; they were obviously constructed without a master plan, at different times, within the available area. Orthogonality and orientation, though, are consistent.

The New Kingdom provides us with the only Egyptian city—Akhetaten—of which the total organic structure has been preserved, but this city was, as we have seen, not typical. It was an artificial foundation hurriedly conceived, quickly built, and short-lived. A look at the map of El Amarna (Fig. 66) makes clear that the city as a whole was not designed in advance. Only the major complexes of temples, palaces, and their dependencies were pre-planned and these only internally according to the principles adhered to in the great monumental structures mentioned earlier. In a few instances, however, the relationships between individual building blocks were considered, as for example in the group formed by the Central Palace, the King's House and the Royal Chapel (Fig. 85). Most buildings are simply juxtaposed within the available space. It will be seen that the same "limited planning" of individual units applies also to the residential districts. The great villas and mansions with their gardens are designed with the same regard for axes, balance and symmetry as the great temples and funerary monuments; the "Clerks' Houses" (Fig. 85) and "Workmen's Village" (Fig. 86), planned and built for special occupancy by a government agency, differ little from the pyramid cities in their efficient double—or single—ribbon layout. Yet in areas not preempted by the official buildings or large townhouses, the population was allowed to build its houses and workshops without the benefit of a master plan or of zoning regulations. As a result irregular agglomerations of houses with hardly recognizable street patterns developed, often so dense that they must be regarded as slums, clearly without any interference by a regulating agency. These characteristics are common to all residential quarters of Akhetaten, the "Main City" (Fig. 87), as well as "Southwestern Quarter" and the "Northern Suburb."

What conclusions can now be drawn as to the layout of a typical city in ancient Egypt? We can assume that one or more walled sacred precinct and a palace or administration building complex formed the nuclei of the town, around which developed the residential and commercial districts, generally not clearly separated. There is no evidence, nor can a logically tenable assumption be made, that Egyptian cities were, as has been suggested, laid out in a geometric, orthogonal or axial pattern. The methodical and expert planning in accordance with definite esthetic principles, as clearly expressed in the monumental mortuary complexes from Saqqara to Deir el Bahari, was apparently applied only to the temple and its temenos and was strictly adhered to throughout the often long periods of building, rebuilding, and enlargement.

The great temple of Amun at Karnak (Fig. 68) is the largest and most famous extant example. From and to the holy precinct led major arteries, "Processional Ways," co-axial with its main axes as at Thebes or Tanis, or at a right angle as at Akhetaten (Fig. 85). It is unlikely that palace complexes were planned as carefully and consistently as temples, if we are to judge by surviving ruins like those of the palace of Amenhotep III at Malqata or of the palaces of Akhenaten at El Amarna, where the established principles of design are hardly carried beyond the individual buildings. It is also highly doubtful that the palace compounds formed part of larger town planning schemes.

We have to visualize the housing and commercial districts of the Egyptian city growing in an indiscriminate way within the available space around temple or palace without pre-planned layout or zoning, similar to the residential quarters contained within the city enclosures and clustered around the temple of Amun at Opet and around the respective sanctuaries of Nekhen and Nekheb.

The great achievements in Egyptian planning were the result of a strong central power with immense resources, which could call upon the most gifted architects and planners to strive for perfection in their tasks. Side by side with this purposeful high-level planning in cases where special interests demanded it, a "laissez faire" attitude prevailed in the absence of such interests.

The vast funerary monuments, temples and palaces, the pyramid cities and fortress towns were the types of construction to which the kings of ancient Egypt paid their main attention and which bear the imprint of directed and controlled planning according to established rules. The great mortuary temple of Ramses III at *Medinet Habu* (Fig. 88) is representative of this planning, in which all these types are combined in one building complex.

THE LEVANT

Confined by the Mediterranean Sea, the Syrian and Arabian Deserts and the Anatolian Mountains, the Levant,* or Syria in its wider sense, forms the central part of the rather heterogenous arch called the "Fertile Crescent," the horns of which are represented by the great river basins of Egypt and Mesopotamia. The Levant was the main link between these early centers of civilization, serving in some periods as a buffer zone and in others as an area of expansion for which the imperialistic powers around it contended. Throughout the course of history it was a coveted prize for the land-hungry nomadic tribes of the desert.

*See maps A and D.

The vast forests of the Lebanon and Mount Amanus were the chief attractions of the otherwise rather poor country. Time and again, by monopolistic trade, diplomacy, or military force, Egyptian and Mesopotamian rulers tried to secure this vital source of timber which they themselves utterly lacked.

At strategic locations along the main routes to Mesopotamia and Egypt, and along the coast where natural harbors offered shelter, prosperous cities developed early in history. Other major settlements and towns sprang up near streams or perennial springs where there was enough arable land to support a larger community, generally built on hills or mountain spurs which could be easily fortified to provide a haven for the population of the surrounding open villages in case of war, which was only too frequent. These cities with their dependencies developed into small city-states under local princes or kinglets, who vied with their neighbors for the enlargement of their own domain but hardly ever acquired the resources to create a large state. In time of foreign domination these petty kings became vassals, at times rivalling each other for personal gain and at others creating coalitions to fight for their freedom.

Innumerable "tellim" or mounds were created by the accumulated occupational debris of successions of destroyed, rebuilt, and again destroyed cities (Fig. 89); many that have been explored and identified (Fig. 90), and many more that still await the spade of the archaeologist bear testimony to the extent of ancient urban settlements.

THE MAIN CITIES

Haleb (Aleppo) and *Alalakh* (Tell Atchana) (Fig. 91) controlled the trade routes from the Euphrates to Mount Amanus and the coast—*Hamath* (Fig. 92) and *Qatna* the road southward from *Aleppo* to the Lebanon; all of these were important Bronze Age cities closely linked culturally to Mesopotamia. *Damascus*, lying in an oasis at the end of the desert road from Mari and athwart one of the chief north-south routes, is one of the oldest continuously occupied cities.

The coastal cities of what became later known as "Phoenicia": *Tyre* (cf. Fig. 7), *Sidon*, and *Byblos* (Gebal) (Fig. 103)—cut off from the hinterland by the Lebanon, and separated from each other by deep ravines—had to rely on seaborne communication and prospered through the export of timber (chiefly to Egypt) and purple dye, and, before the rise of Greek competition, through a monopoly of the maritime trade and the construction of ocean-going ships. *Ugarit* (Ras Shamra) farther north, with its harbor of Minet el Beida was the most important Bronze Age center of commerce on the Mediterranean seaboard, trading with Cyprus and the Aegean, Egypt, Mesopotamia, and Anatolia.

The chief cities of the land of Canaan, later called Palestine after the Philistines, occupied strategic positions along the main highways through the country. *Hazor* (Fig. 93) dominated the routes from Galilee to Damascus and into the Leontes and Orontes valleys; the strong fortress cities of *Megiddo* (Fig. 90), *Taanach*, and *Bethshan* the trunk roads leading through the Plain of Jezreel; *Tirzah, Shechem, Bethel*, and *Ai* (Fig. 99) the roads across the central hill country of Samaria. *Jerusalem* (Fig. 94) controlled the only road from the Jordan valley through the hills of Judah and the road from Samaria to the south via Hebron. The approaches to the "Shephelah," the Judaean foothills, were guarded by the fortified towns of *Debir* (Tell Beit Mirsim) (Fig. 116), *Eglon* (Tell el Hesi), *Lachish* (Tell ed Duweir) (Fig. 95), *Bethshemesh* (Ain Shems), and *Gezer*. The strong cities of *Gaza, Ashkelon* (Fig. 4), *Ashdod*, and *Ekron* lay on the main highway to Egypt in the coastal strip later occupied by the Philistines. *Jericho's* (Fig. 96) early importance was due to its control of the main route across the Jordan into the heart of Canaan. *Dibon, Rabbath-Ammon*, and *Ashtaroth*, finally, developed along the caravan route across the trans-Jordanian plateau from Egypt and Arabia into northern Syria.

NEOLITHIC CITIES

The recent excavations of Jericho have uncovered the earliest urban settlement in the history of mankind discovered so far, dated by the carbon-14 method to the Eighth Millennium B.C. The town designated as "Pre-Pottery Neolithic A" developed over a mound of occupational debris more than 4 m. in height covering an area of not less than 4 hectares. It was fortified by a strong stone wall. Traces of curvilinear houses of the period have been found.

In the Seventh Millennium B.C. newcomers with a fully developed type of architecture—which implies an urban development somewhere else as yet unknown—built a new town on the site, "Pre-Pottery Neolithic B," with rectilinear houses consisting of several rather large rooms arranged around courtyards, and shrines. This town spread over an area larger than Bronze Age Jericho, but no plan of it can be reconstructed as yet. At a rather late stage it was surrounded by a massive stone wall. These spectacular urban developments must indicate the existence of an advanced agriculture based on irrigation and of extensive trade.

EARLY BRONZE AGE CITIES

With the destruction of the Neolithic B town of Jericho a retrogression set in and no urban settlement is known in the Levant until the Early Bronze Age. Successive invasions, mainly from the east by new groups recognizable by their distinctive pottery and tombs, led to a progressive settlement of the country. Many of the villages of this "Proto-Urban" period become the nuclei of important Bronze Age cities. At the beginning of the Third Millennium B.C. a whole series of walled cities are to be found across the country, modest in size but reasonably prosperous, of a comparatively uniform culture—small city-states in strong rivalry with each other.

The excavations of the Early Bronze Age levels have been up to now too spotty to allow a study of town planning, but certain characteristics can be established from the evidence available. The towns appear to have been fully developed before defensive ramparts were deemed necessary. These were high and massive, many meters thick, built of mud-brick or unworked stones, and they were strengthened by earth embankments as at Tirzah (north wall) and *Beth Yerah,* or by additional walls built directly against the original wall as at Jericho, or at some distance from it as at Ai (Fig. 97), Taanach, and Tirzah. Semicircular towers in the fortification walls are known from *Arad* (Fig. 98), Jericho and Ai (Fig. 99), square towers from Byblos (Fig. 100). At Megiddo (Stratum XVIII) (Fig. 101) there is for the first time evidence of an ambitious town planning scheme. An originally steeply inclined hill-town quarter is replaced by a series of level terraces (Fig. 102) with well-planned streets and square houses, a sanctuary and a large, probably public, building.

Early Bronze Age dwellings as uncovered at Jericho, Tirzah, Ai (Fig. 99), and Arad (Fig. 98) were generally well built, of rectangular shape, and mostly oriented north-south. Only a few complete city quarters have been excavated. In Byblos (Fig. 103), detailed excavation plans of an urban section show a development from its earliest stage c. 3000 B.C. to its destruction during the First Intermediate period. Narrow twisting streets and access alleys separate irregular agglomerations of houses which, however, consist generally of rectangular rooms. A large public building and the earliest temple of the "Ba'alat Gebal" (II on the plan) lie southwest of the main street.

In Hamath (Fig. 92), a succession of excavated levels from the end of the Early Bronze Age gives a picture of increasing density of the built-up town area. The originally free-standing houses grow through uncontrolled additions of rooms and whole dwellings until the open spaces around them are reduced to narrow zigzagging thoroughfares and blind alleys, yet rooms tend to retain a rectangular shape and a uniform orientation. All Early Bronze Age cities came to a violent end at about the same time toward the close of the Third Millennium B.C., when a complete break in urban civilization occurred. The Amorites, nomads from the Arabian Desert, overran Palestine and Syria, invaded Egypt to bring about the fall of the VI Dynasty, and infiltrated into Mesopotamia to contribute ultimately to the end of Sumerian independence.

After a cultural recession that lasted about three hundred years (Intermediate Early Bronze-Middle Bronze period, 2300–2000 B.C.) a new urban civilization emerged throughout the Levant,—the "Canaanite."

MIDDLE BRONZE AGE CITIES

Evidence of newly built towns, fully developed and surrounded by strong walls, which can be dated to the beginning of the Middle Bronze Age (c. 2000 B.C.) has been found at all major sites.

During the later Middle Bronze Age (c. 1900–1500 B.C.) an unprecedented growth of these cities took place and many new towns sprang up, most of them reaching an extent never to be attained again, in spite of continued upheavals that are attested by several levels of destruction and subsequent rebuilding. Some cities outgrew their original fortified hill-town and spread out over an enormous area at its foot, which was then surrounded by new ramparts. Qatna reached an area of about 100 hectares; Hazor (Fig. 93) grew from 10 hectares to a city of more than 80.9 hectares with a probable population of 30,000. A similar development occurred at Ugarit, Alalakh and *Carchemish* (Fig. 138). The cities were well planned with large public buildings, shops, stores and workshops; they were provided with drainage systems and cobbled streets. The comparative well-being of the cities is revealed by large amounts of imported pottery and luxury articles.

This prosperity of the Levantine lands during the Middle Bronze Age seems to have been due to the relative political stability, lasting about 200 years, effected by a new power which, by the middle of the eighteenth century B.C., had established its domination from the upper Euphrates to the Nile—a vast trade area. These Hyksos or "rulers of foreign lands," as the Egyptians called them, were a heterogeneous group of nomadic tribes of Semitic and Indo-European origin who have left as permanent evidence of their rule a completely new type of fortification that can be found in all major cities of Palestine and Syria. This consisted of great artificial embankments that were built against the lower slopes of the city-mound and were generally preceded by a moat. Their crest supported the peripheral city-wall of mud-brick. At the end of the era these ramparts gave way to battered walls of polygonal stone as found at Jericho (Fig. 104), Shechem and Hazor.

The Hyksos rampart has been convincingly linked to the introduction of the battering ram; similarly, a new type of city-gate (which also had antecedents in Mesopotamia) was made necessary by another revolutionary change in warfare: the use of battle chariots. The L-shaped gate, unsuitable for vehicular traffic, still in use at the beginning of the period, as discovered at Megiddo (Stratum XIII) (Fig. 105) and Tirzah, was superseded by a gate of straight approach with multiple internal barriers and flanked by massive towers (Fig. 106).

Coherent sections of Middle Bronze II city quarters have been excavated at Jericho (Fig. 107), Debir (Fig. 108), and Hazor. All are rather densely built up, with few open spaces. Streets are paved and drained. Houses continue to be basically rectangular and oriented roughly north-south. In Jericho and Debir, evidence has been found of upper stories which served as living quarters; the lower stories were used as stables, storerooms, and workshops. Single-room shops appear in Jericho. One large patrician house was found in Debir (Fig. 108).

LATE BRONZE AGE CITIES

Levels of destruction in nearly all cities bear testimony to the Egyptian conquest of the country by the kings of the XVIII Dynasty (fifteenth century B.C.). Some, like Jericho and Debir, remained unoccupied for a considerable time. In general, the period of Egyptian domination was one of oppression and exploitation, and the Late Bronze Age cities, with some exceptions, show lack of systematic planning, poor construction, and a decrease in wealth and culture (Fig. 109).

Unlike the Palestinian cities, the city-states of northern Syria continued to flourish through the Late Bronze Age, though under varying suzerainty. Some sections of the city quarters in the northeastern part of Ugarit (Fig. 110) have been excavated. One, between the temples of Ba'al (I) and Dagon (II), east, contains a library, schools, and a priests' quarter; it seems to have been specially planned as a cult center with nearly parallel streets and north-south orientation. The residential quarters around this section show a less regular layout and no consistent orientation, but the houses are well built, with numerous rooms, an upper story, sanitary installation, and individual wells.

The vast palace complex of Ugarit (Fig. 111) on the northwestern edge of the mound gives evidence of the power and wealth concentrated in the hands of a feudal lord, merchant prince, and head of a prosperous city-state in the Late Bronze Age. Eighty-five rooms around six courtyards have been excavated so far and an extensive archive discovered. The palace, which served not only as residence for the king but also as government administration and business center, was not planned as a whole, but grew by the agglomeration reminiscent of Mesopotamian palaces.

Only the northwestern section of the mound of Alalakh (Fig. 91) has been excavated, probably representing the acropolis of a Bronze Age town which spread at its foot. Surrounded by a massive wall, it appears carefully planned. The citadel with its gates and parade ground, the palace, temple, and a quarter of large residence buildings are all equally oriented and of rectangular layout. Streets intersect the peripheral ring road at right angles. The late fifteenth-century palace of Niqmepa, on the other hand, was built without regard to the earlier plan beneath it—at odd angles with the previous buildings. A residential quarter (Fig. 112) from the end of the period (Fig. 112) shows a substantial number of houses with rectangular rooms, combined in large city blocks.

THE IRON AGE

Archaeological findings bear out most of the account of the conquest of Canaan by the Israelites. There is clear evidence of the destruction of the cities of the Shephelah, Lachish, Eglon, and Debir, and of the end of the great Galilean city of Hazor in the thirteenth century B.C. The Israelites were not strong enough to take the fortified cities by assault; they used cunning instead, according to the biblical account, and they avoided the fortress cities of the Plain of Jezreel—Bethshan, Taanach and Megiddo, as well as Gezer in the south; nor could they take the Yebusite fortress of Jerusalem. Other cities, like Shechem, they infiltrated and took over gradually.

While the Israelite conquest affected only a part of Palestine, the whole of the Levant fell victim to a catastrophic disruption of its civilization: the migration and invasion of the so-called Peoples of the Sea at the beginning of the twelfth century B.C., who, driven out from the Aegean, attacked by land and by sea the whole eastern Mediterranean seaboard from Anatolia to Egypt. The Hittite Empire was annihilated and all the great cities of northern Syria—Carchemish, Alalakh, Aleppo and Ugarit—fell before their onslaught; although Ramses III finally (c. 1175) repulsed their advance on the Egyptian coast he could not stop them from settling on the Levantine coast. One group occupied the Lebanese shore where, after the destruction of Sidon and Tyre, it settled among the Canaanite inhabitants. The assimilation of the two peoples resulted in the rise of a new nation, the Phoenicians, with a culture of their own. A larger group, the Philistines, seized the southern coastland, captured and destroyed its cities and then rebuilt them. They also became assimilated with the local Canaanite population. Their state centered around five principal cities: Gaza, Ashkelon, Ashdod, Ekron and *Gath*, each independent under its overlord but allied in case of war. Finally, during the twelfth century, a third group of peoples—the Aramaeans—invaded Syria from the east, expanding both into what was originally Hittite territory to the north and threatening Israelite lands in the south.

IRON AGE CITIES

The Israelites built their small towns in the unoccupied hill country, the settlement of which was made possible by the invention of cisterns waterproofed with lime plaster. In the Canaanite cities in which they settled after their conquest—often only in a small area of the original Bronze Age city—they repaired the city walls in patchwork fashion and put up agglomerations of crude rubble-built houses around small central courtyards, which served to accommodate their patriarchal family units. There were no planned streets or sewers. Such town quarters were found at Ai (Fig. 113), Hazor and Bethel. Their standardized houses at Tirzah (Fig. 114) show an advance in planning.

Only in the tenth century B.C. under the reign of King David (c. 1000–961 B.C.) was a concerted effort made by the Israelites to develop a system of fortification and city planning of their own. The new walls were built according to the casemate system used earlier by the Hittites.

Following the line of the rampart a 16 to 20 m. peripheral strip of houses was built up at right angles to it, separated by a ring road from the central city area which was occupied by irregular agglomerations of houses that were generally oriented north-south and were provided with a rudimentary system of streets. The dwellings were poorly built and there is no evidence of important public buildings. Bethshemesh (II) (Fig. 115), Megiddo (V), Debir (B3) (Fig. 116), and Mizpah are good examples of Israelite Iron Age cities.

The comparative weakness of the great powers Egypt and Assyria enabled the Israelite kingdom temporarily to dominate the Levant and enjoy a short-lived prosperity manifested in unprecedented building activity. King David had crushed the Philistine power and had subdued the rivaling Aramaean state of Damascus. He had also succeeded in finding a neutral capital for the quarreling and envious northern and southern Israelite tribes and in providing a political and spiritual center for the United Kingdom—Jerusalem.

Jebusite Jerusalem lay on the southeastern spur of a mountain which extended through a narrow neck from a main ridge farther north (Fig. 117). The hill of Ophel was surrounded in the west by the Central Valley, in the south by the Valley of Hinnom, and in the east by the deep Kidron Valley and was made nearly impregnable by strong fortifications.

David succeeded in taking the city, made it his royal capital and had a palace built by Phoenician craftsmen. But it remained for Solomon (c. 961–922 B.C.) to build the Temple and an ambitious residential complex on a series of vast terraces north of the city of David (Fig. 118), the link to which he broadened by a large fill operation (the biblical "Millo") and then provided with a guard tower and an extension of the city walls (Fig. 117).

The Bible is specific about some other building enterprises of Solomon: He "built Hazor, Megiddo and Gezer," and also "cities for his chariots, horsemen, and stores" across the country. Archaeological evidence has borne out these statements. Hazor (Fig. 93) had not been occupied since its Late Bronze Age destruction, and Solomon built a new city on the original tell. Casemate walls with nearly identical triple gateways flanked by two towers (Fig. 119), built of carefully dressed ashlar, indicate the common planning of all three cities mentioned.

The far-flung enterprises of Solomon, the cost of his central administration, and his strong standing army led to high taxes and oppression. While before the establishment of the monarchy the Israelite society had been classless in contrast to the Canaanite, a clear distinction between classes now became apparent. Merchants and officials stood in sharp contrast to the impoverished mass of agricultural and other workers.

This change in social conditions becomes manifest in Tirzah where the uniform dwellings of the tenth century B.C. gave way to a juxtaposition of large private houses of superior construction taking the place of several small earlier buildings and some rather poor houses; there even appears an ample, well-to-do quarter separated by a wall from a crowded shabby quarter. After Solomon's death the northern states revolted against the oppression by Rehoboam, and Jeroboam became king of the new state of Israel while the southern kingdom of Judah remained under the Davidic house. The Davidic empire collapsed and the Aramaeans, Ammonites and Moabites seceded and formed independent states.

Samaria was planned as capital of the Northern Kingdom on a grand scale intended to compete with Jerusalem. The whole summit of the hill (Fig. 120) was turned into a huge rectangular terrace by means of retaining walls, built of carefully drafted ashlar. A well-planned palace and a great courtyard belong to the same building period of Omri (876–869 B.C.). Ahab (c. 869–850 B.C.) extended the terrace to the north and west by the addition of a new retaining and fortification wall, this time of the casemate type, while in the south the existing wall was reinforced.

A palace complex for the Israelite governor in Megiddo (IV) (Fig. 121) with a large courtyard and enclosure wall, and a citadel in Hazor (VIII) show the same kind of ambitious planning typical of the Omri Dynasty and bear again evidence of Phoenician craftsmanship. At Megiddo (Fig. 121) the whole fortified hilltop was turned into a citadel with administration and government buildings and stable compounds. The population seems to have been relegated to a lower city enclosed by a secondary wall.

In the late tenth and ninth centuries the casemate walls were superseded in many cities by massive stone walls with salients and recesses, probably in order to offer better resistance to a new type of battering ram. Examples may be found in Megiddo (IV), Hazor (VIII), Mizpah (Fig. 122), and Lachish (Fig. 95).

In the eighth century B.C., before the Assyrian campaigns, most of the Israelite cities seem to have reached their maximal population, with houses densely crowded within the walls and overflowing beyond them.

A new type of city plan, unique for Palestine, appears after the Assyrian conquest in Megiddo (II) (Fig. 123), probably due to transplanted settlers: a system of regular insulae oriented north-south with an orthogonal street layout.

The ingenious solutions for the water supply to the hill-cities of Palestine must be singled out as the greatest achievement of planning in the Levant. In the Early Bronze Age city of Arad and the Late Iron Age city of Lachish, for instance, the runoff from a whole mountainside was collected in a huge catch basin. In Bethshemesh and Debir wells were dug deep down into the rock to reach the ground water level, and in Gezer, *Gibeon*, Megiddo and Jerusalem (Fig. 124), to mention a few other examples, long tunnels were cut through solid rock (Fig. 125) to provide a protected access to a fountain at the foot of the town hill outside the walls.

In short, it may be stated that the ancient cities of the Levant grew out of earlier settlements in relatively defensible locations, where a reliable source of water was available, in a rather haphazard and uncontrolled manner. Planning initially was limited to the ramparts, the water supply, the temple and the palace. More comprehensive town planning schemes date in Syria mainly from the Late Bronze Age and in Palestine from the Solomonic period.

ANATOLIA AND THE SYRIAN FOOTHILLS

The peninsula of Asia Minor, called "Anatolia"* (Orient) by the Greeks, forms a vast bridge between the two continents that was crossed in the course of history by hosts of migrating peoples in either direction. But while eastern, southern, and central Anatolia were closely tied to the Asiatic mainland and were strongly affected by the ancient eastern civilization, western and northern Anatolia were exposed to a predominant influence from the west: Thessaly, Thrace, and the Aegean world.

The cultural divisions of Asia Minor, as well as its political fragmentation, were mainly due to the nature of its topography. Mountain ranges enclose the central highland on all sides, the Pontic Mountains in the north, the East Aegean Mountains in the west, and the Taurus and Anti-Taurus in the south, while the mountains of eastern Anatolia merge with the mountain chains radiating from the Armenian massif. Only the coastal regions and seaward mountain slopes receive ample rainfall and are suitable for intensive cultivation. The entire extent of the interior, with an extremely dry continental climate, is a steppe that can support only seasonal grazing, with large areas of desert and barren rocky mountains which in antiquity were probably still covered by scrub. A few larger rivers, none navigable, break through the mountain barriers and reach the sea. Near these rivers, where water was adequate and the soil fertile, agriculture and animal husbandry developed at an early period.

The Taurus and the Pontic Mountains were rich in ores of copper, silver, and iron, and by the end of the Third Millennium B.C., copper was a major export article to Mesopotamia, traded against textiles and tin, which was not available in Anatolia and was essential for the production of bronze. The discovery of a great number of clay tablets with correspondence in cuneiform script pertaining to the business activities of Assyrian merchants and their establishment of trading posts revealed much about the commerce between Mesopotamia and Anatolia from the twentieth to the seventeenth century B.C. Assyrian merchant

*See map A.

colonies called "Karums" have been excavated in Kanesh, Hattusas and near Alishar; others are mentioned in letters.

The main trade routes into Anatolia led from Mesopotamia along the Tigris and Euphrates via Malatya or Marash across the Anti-Taurus to Kanesh and thence to Hattusas; from northern Syria through the Syrian Gates across the Amanus or via the Cilician Gates across the Taurus into the Anatolian plateau; from Iran through Armenia to the central highland.

ÇATAL HÜYÜK AND HACILAR

Excavations of recent years have proven that the first large neolithic settlements and urban centers did not develop in the great river plains, as previously assumed. After the discovery of the neolithic town of Jericho, dated by radio-carbon measurements to the Eighth Millennium B.C., an even larger neolithic town site covering 13 hectares has been found in southern Anatolia and has been explored in depth over a limited area. The twelve bared levels of *Çatal Hüyük*, which was situated on a small river in the plain of Konya, date from the middle of the Seventh to the middle of the Sixth Millennium B.C. Level VIB (Fig. 126) from about 6000 B.C. shows a dense cluster of irregularly rectangular, contiguous one-story houses built of mud-brick and entered by ladders from the roofs which served as streets and followed in steps the slope of the mountain.

At *Hacilar*, another neolithic site of long occupation, about 300 km. to the west, the last levels before its ultimate destruction reveal incipient urban planning in the fortified settlements IIA and I (Fig. 127), dating from about 5400 and 5200 B.C. respectively, which are also only excavated in part. Here, the houses within the enclosures are arranged around a number of courtyards but they show an agglomeration of contiguous irregularly shaped units similar to Çatal Hüyük. To date, these early towns appear isolated in time and culture and cannot be linked to any later development in Asia Minor.

All sites in Central Anatolia excavated so far feature destruction levels dating to the beginning of the Second Millennium when the Indo-European Hittites invaded and conquered the land, but too little has come to light yet of the destroyed Hattian cities to know what they were like. At the time of the arrival of the Assyrian merchants the country was divided into a number of small principalities, and the names of their capital cities, such as *Hatti* (Hattusas), *Nesa* (probably identical with Kanesh), *Kussara*, *Zalpuva*, *Salitavara* and *Purushanda*, are mentioned in documents, but to date only Hattusas and Kanesh have been identified.

KANESH (KÜLTEPE)

The ancient city of Kanesh occupied a strategic position between

Mount Argaeus (Erciyas Dagh) and the Halys River, not far from the later city of *Caesarea* (Kayseri); it controlled the main Anatolian caravan routes. The oval mound of *Kültepe* (450 by 550 m.) (Fig. 128), the traces of its outer ramparts still recognizable, has not yet been systematically excavated, but unfortunately it has been severely damaged by indiscriminate digging.

East of the city and around its walls spread the nearly autonomous foreign merchants' colony and trading center, the "Karum" (Fig. 129), which has been extensively explored and its three main occupation levels from the twentieth to the seventeenth century B.C. recorded. While size, layout, and quality of the houses vary from level to level— from two to a great number of generally rectangular rooms usually with an open front-court and upper floor—the buildings on all levels from nearly continuous clusters forcing the narrow streets to zigzag around, a peculiarity which we will recognize as being typical of Anatolian residential quarters.

ALISHAR

The city of Alishar was situated in a fertile plain watered by a tributary of the Halys, slightly east of the main route from Kanesh to Hattusas. Today the site is occupied by a low oval mound (Fig. 130) covering an area of 11.3 hectares which is dominated in the west by the steep tell of the citadel rising to a height of 40 m. above the level of the valley. While the settlement of Alishar goes back to the Fourth Millennium B.C., the city reached its apogee at the time of the Hittite Empire. The citadel, constructed earlier, with a strong fortification wall and S-shape gateway, was retained by the Hittites without change. The outer city enclosure, which can be dated to the first half of the second Millennium B.C., represents an early type of a Hittite casemate wall.

As far as the excavated areas of Alishar allow any conclusions, there existed a system of radial streets, ring roads, and a defense road along the outer rampart. The dwellings themselves form again irregular amorphous agglomerations, although the single rooms are mostly rectangular.

HATTUSAS (BOGAZKÖY)

The name of Hatti (Hattusas) appears first on the Kültepe tablets as that of the seat of a petty king of an Anatolian city to which an Assyrian "Karum" is attached. About 1600 B.C. Hattusas was chosen by Hattusilis I as the Hittite capital instead of the former residence city of Kussara.

The strategic location of this new capital in the center of the great bend of the Halys in the Hittite heartland and on the main trade routes across northern Anatolia was eminently suited for the control of the region. The city (Fig. 131) occupied a rocky massif surrounded on three sides by deep ravines and therefore needed strong fortification only along the southern, more gradual slopes. The old lower city situated on the northern spur of the mountain was guarded in the south by a deep gully and protected at the southeast by the high rock of the Büyükkale, an ideal emplacement for the citadel. At the beginning of the fourteenth century B.C., a new upper city was added to the south, and the area of the capital was nearly quadrupled to 168 hectares.

The layout of the city does not follow a standard type nor was it conceived as a whole. Instead each separate quarter was adapted by the Hittite city-builders in masterly fashion to the peculiarities of the site, and the fortifications were skillfully planned to take advantage of its topographical features. The citadel as well as each city quarter and castle were protected by their own enclosure, the city as a whole by a double curtain wall with towers, double gateways, and postern gates for sallies by the defenders.

The center of the lower city was occupied by the large temenos with a temple complex of the Weather God (I), tutelary deity of Hattusas, dating in its final form from c. 1400 B.C. A second holy precinct with four temples was situated on a plateau at the extreme south of the new upper city. The temples, which have no common orientation, seem to have been related to a processional street skirting the whole city, and leading to a sanctuary across the ravine.

During the time of the Empire the citadel (Fig. 132) served as residence and administrative center for the Hittite Great Kings. Like the city itself, it does not follow a unified building concept. The only apparent principle in the layout is the clever utilization of the site conditions. On the highest level in the northeast probably stood the residence palace, of which little remains. Around it, following the contours, were grouped a number of isolated structures, extant mostly only in their foundation walls, which have been interpreted as royal apartments (F), guest house (E), audience hall (D), shrine (C), service building (H), official residence (G), and portico and guard house (B). The approach road from the main gate skirted the western wall and led between buildings E and D to the upper terrace. A large assembly court occupied the lower terrace off the gate.

Two main levels of a residential quarter in the old city north of the temenos have been uncovered, which might be called typical (Figs. 133, 134). As in Anatolian examples already mentioned, the house units of both levels are clustered together, wall to wall, in irregular configurations. Crooked alleyways of minimal width, paved and provided with drains, were left open to give access to the dwellings.

The greatest and most influential achievements of the Hittite city-builders were their fortifications (Fig. 135). Planned with supreme skill, technical knowledge and engineering ingenuity, they were constructed in gigantic cyclopean stone masonry with a mud-brick superstructure. Hittite city walls, gates (Fig. 136), and posterns (Fig. 137) were never surpassed in their rugged monumentality.

44

At the end of the thirteenth century B.C. the Hittite Empire succumbed to the attacks by the "Sea-Peoples." All cities excavated so far show their violent end by conflagration. But while in Anatolia a complete cultural break occurs with the advent of the Phrygians, Hittite culture lingers on in the mountain regions bordering the north Syrian plain where a few successor states carry on a precarious independent existence under increasing cultural and political pressure by Aramaeans and Assyrians until they are absorbed by the Assyrian Empire during the ninth or eighth century B.C.

The early importance of Carchemish (Fig. 138) was due to its control of the river traffic and the trade routes across the Euphrates. The city had already been incorporated into the Hittite Empire in the middle of the Second Millennium B.C., ruled as a vassal state by royal princes. Overrun by the Sea-Peoples, it was soon rebuilt and it enjoyed unprecedented prosperity as an independent principality. The construction of a new outer town more than doubled the original area, but the few isolated houses excavated give us no clue to its layout. We can only say that the double outer enclosure of irregular polygonal shape combines the Hittite principle of utilization of topography with Assyrian rectilinear forms.

An idea about Neo-Hittite planning may be obtained, however, from the only excavated section of the rebuilt inner city (Fig. 139) of the tenth and ninth centuries B.C. As in Hittite architecture, symmetry is confined to gates and porches. A triangular plaza opening off the street leading to the Water Gate is reminiscent of the square off the access road to the Büyükkale. But the seemingly odd siting of the temple established a sophisticated relationship with the main approaches, which are cleverly utilized for the placement of the famous orthostat (wall revetment) reliefs. For one ascending the street from the Water Gate, the view is directed to the curving Herald's Wall and beyond it; then, unexpectedly, the vista opens up but is confined by the Long Wall. The eye of anyone descending the Great Staircase is guided by the Long Wall toward the Herald's Wall and then by its curve to the right. For one passing through the King's Gate the temple closes the square in front of it visually but leads the eye beyond it.

The citadel mound (Fig. 140) marks the site of the earliest settlements and towns of Carchemish. The oval inner town dating to the middle of the Hittite period is enclosed on the river side by a zigzagging wall of Hittite origin with some casemates, but on the other sides by a Hyksos-type earth rampart and ditch.

The fortified towns of *Guzana*, *Hadatu* and *Til Barsip*, lie on the main caravan road from Assyria to Syria via Nineveh, Harran and Aleppo. *Til Barsip* (Tell Ahmar) (Fig. 141) served as royal capital of the Aramaean state of Bit Adini before its conquest by Shalmaneser III in 856 B.C. A semicircular rampart of 1100 m. diameter, consisting of double wall, enclosed the city on three sides; the south side was protected by the steep embankment of the Euphrates. Only an Assyrian palace on the citadel mound overlooking the river and an Aramaean palace compound beneath it have been excavated.

Also in *Hadatu* (Arslan Tash) (Fig. 142) only a late Assyrian palace of Tiglath-Pileser III (744–727 B.C.), and a slightly earlier palace where a hoard of ivory was found, have been unearthed. The oval town wall of 2 km. in circumference with bastions and three gates, dating probably only from the eighth century B.C., has been traced in its entirety.

Occupying a strategic position comparable to those of Carchemish and Til Barsip, the citadel of *Guzana* (Tell Halaf) (Fig. 143) rose on a high terrace above the Khabur River. On a lower level around it spread the town, protected in the north by the river and on the other sides by fortification walls with bastions. It was built according to Assyrian town planning principles in rectangular shape and covered an area of 60.8 hectares. The main town gate in the south led directly to the citadel with its government buildings, residence palaces and the famous ceremonial palace of Kapara. Guzana flourished as an independent principality in the tenth and ninth centuries B.C. but became an Assyrian provincial capital in 808 B.C.

Sam'al (Zinçirli) (Fig. 144) lay at the northern foot of Mount Amanus on the route from Syria into Anatolia via Marash. It was enclosed by two concentric circular walls, each provided with a hundred rectangular towers and entered through equally spaced double gateways of which the strongest in the south led to the citadel which rose on a mound slightly off the center of the city. The citadel, protected by its own strong wall with round towers and accessible by two sets of gates set between massive square towers, was divided into four zones on different levels by secondary walls, reminiscent of the arrangement at Hattusas. Four palaces with their dependencies and a barracks complex occupied the upper levels. The town itself, which covered an area of 36.8 hectares, has not been explored. In 727 B.C. Sam'al was incorporated into the Assyrian Empire after less than two hundred years of independent existence.

Anatolian cities seem to have been planned primarily with their defense in mind. They were built in strategic locations, with a minimal, oval or polygonal defense perimeter and skillful utilization of the natural topographical features. Their residential quarters grew mainly uncontrolled by organic agglomeration. Neo-Hittite cities show a marked Assyrian influence in their layout, with a tendency to geometrization.

46

ARMENIA AND PERSIA

1. URARTU*

The mountains of Kurdistan, which gird the plain of Northern Mesopotamia in a huge arc between the Zagros Mountains in the east and
the Eastern Taurus in the west, are but the foothills of the vast massif of
Armenia that is crowned by the lofty peak of Ararat of biblical fame.
Broken up into a succession of mountain ranges, valleys, and ravines,
the massif both links and separates the Iranian Plateau and the Anatolian
Highland, and it interposes itself as a formidable barrier between the
region of the Caspian and Black Seas and Mesopotamia. Access into
this high and rugged mountain area is provided by the valleys of the
great rivers: Euphrates, Tigris, Upper Zab, Araxes, and Kura. The most
important direct trade routes from Iran into Anatolia, to the Black Sea
shore, and thence to the west, passed through the mountain valleys of
Armenia.

The chronicles of kings Shalmaneser I (1274–1245 B.C.) and Tiglath-
Pileser I (1116–1078 B.C.) tell us of Assyrian wars against the "Nairi"
lands in the mountains north of Assyria, one of which is called "Uruatri."
By the time of the reign of Shalmaneser III (858–825 B.C.) the hitherto
independent tribes of the region appear to have united under a King
Arame (c. 880–844 B.C.). His capital city of *Arsashkun*, which stood
northeast of Lake Van, could not resist the Assyrian attackers, and was
destroyed. Under Sardur I (c. 835–825 B.C.) a strong Urartian kingdom
was developed around *Tuspa*, the newly founded and fortified capital
east of Lake Van. Menua, Argistis I, and Sardur II extended the domination to the Kura in the north, the Euphrates in the west, and the Upper
Diyala in the southeast during the following century. Thus Urartu became a major power posing a direct threat to Assyrian supremacy. The
victorious campaigns of Tiglath-Pileser III (744–727 B.C.) and Sargon II (721–705 B.C.) attacking from the south, and onslaughts from
the north by the Cimmerians and then by the Scythians finally brought
Urartu's independence to an end, after little more than two hundred
years of existence.

With great effort, patience, and skill as well as unlimited manpower,
the Urartian kings succeeded in making their rugged and inhospitable
mountain country suitable for cultivation, habitation, and an advanced
culture with particular excellence in engineering and metalwork. They
took great pride in their newly built cities, their citadels and fortresses,
their dams and irrigation canals (often tunnelled through sheer rock),
and their fields, orchards and vineyards which were planted on carefully
constructed terraces along the steep mountain slopes. We gain a vivid
picture of the fruits of this persistent endeavor from the fragments of

*See map A.

47

Sargon II's description of the events of his eighth campaign in 714 B.C. He relates:

> The city of Ulhu, a stronghold at the foot of Mount Kishpai... they did not drink, they did not satisfy their hunger... Ursa (Rusa I), their king and counsellor... showed them where the water gushed forth, a ditch carrying these flowing waters, he dug, a ... brought plenty like the Euphrates. He made numberless channels lead off from its bed... and irrigated orchards. Its wasteland, which from days old... and made fruit and grapes as abundant as rain. Plane trees... like a forest... The ground of his uncultivated area he made like a meadow, flooding it abundantly in spring time...
> A palace, a royal dwelling, he built by the side of the river for his enjoyment. With cypress beams he roofed it... the city of Sharduri-Hurda, a fortress, for his defense.
>
> Luckenbill, *Ancient Records* II, 160

None of the larger cities has yet been found. Many of the cities mentioned in the annals were probably, like *Musasir*, destroyed. However, a number of fortress towns have been systematically surveyed, though not completely excavated.

Kefkalessi (Fig. 145), discovered northwest of Lake Van, was probably a typical fortress town. It closely resembles the description of such towns in the Assyrian annals:

> Strong cities... they stood on the peaks... mighty fortifications... high walls surrounding their sides... great palaces... were spread out... lookouts... towers were constructed on the summit of the mountain....
>
> Luckenbill, *Ancient Records II*, 163

Although the town area has not yet been excavated and much of the citadel and the buttressed enclosure wall has been destroyed, we can discern the "lookout tower," connected by a double protective wall to a citadel occupying the highest ground above the city. This citadel was surrounded by a strong, zigzagging wall which skillfully exploited the topographical features of the hilltop.

The same planning principle is evident in the remains of the fortress town of *Tesebaini* (Karmir Blur or "Red Hill") (Fig. 146) which was probably founded by Menua in the late ninth century and built in its final shape by Rusall (680–654 B.C.). To date, only the citadel (Fig. 147), covering an area of nearly 1.4 hectares, has been excavated in its entirety. It was constructed in a strategic location, on a high promontory protected on two sides by the gorge of the river Zanga, a tributary of the Araxes. The massive fortification walls follow the contour of the escarpment above the river. The inner walls of the citadel, which face on a large court, and the outer walls, which look out over the city, are all provided with buttresses and guarded by strong square towers. Internally the citadel consists of a maze of rectangular, generally elongated rooms with very heavy mud-brick walls. Most of the rooms were used for

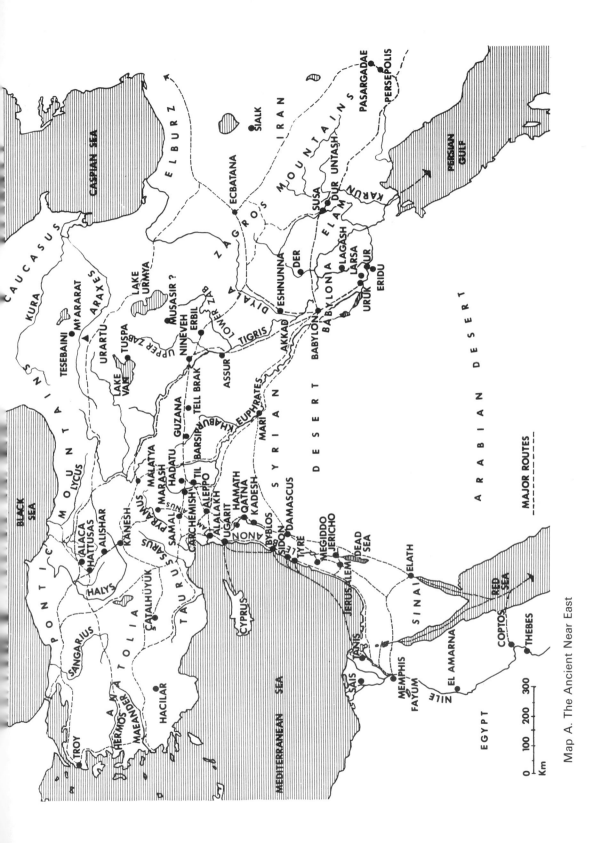

Map A. The Ancient Near East

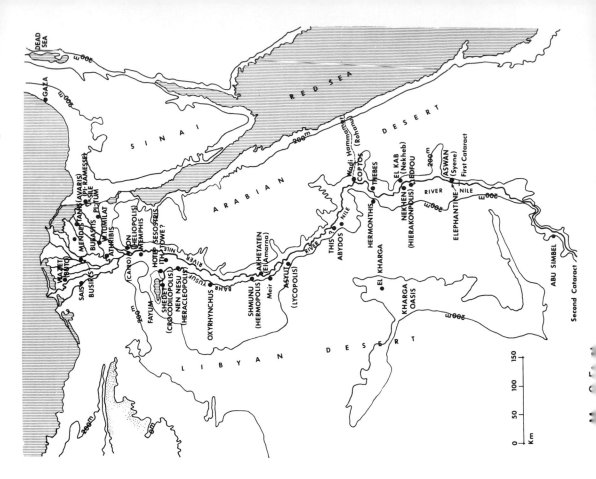
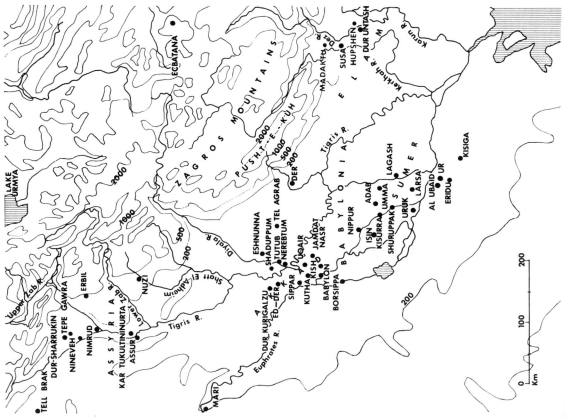

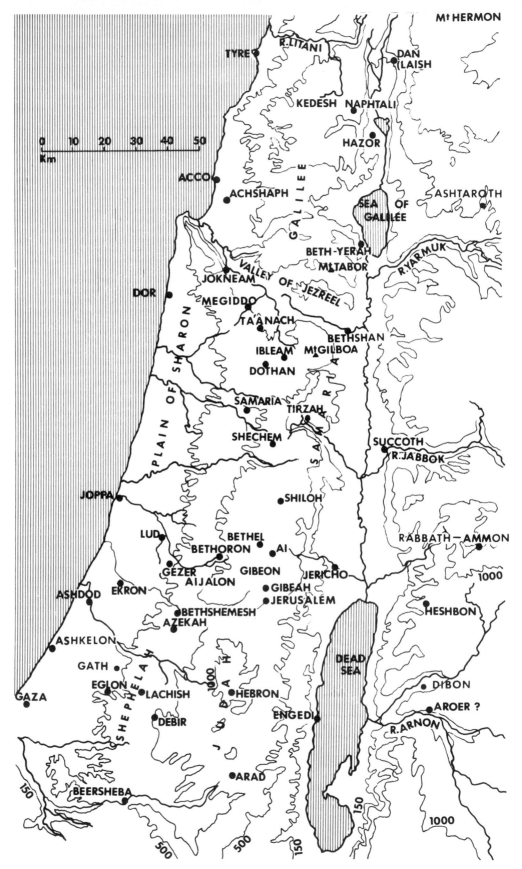

Map D. Palestine

1. Ur. The city with its ziggurat. Model. Time of Ur-Nammu, 2112–2095.
2. Slate palette of King Narmer, I Dynasty of Egypt.
3. The Egyptian border, fortress of Sile. Relief of Sethos I, 1303–1290, in the Temple of Karnak.
4. The city of Ashkelon in Southern Palestine. Relief of Ramses II, 1290–1224, in the Temple of Karnak.

5. The Syrian fortress city of Kadesh on the Orontes. Relief of Ramses II, 1290–1224, at Abu Simbel.
6. Sketch plan of Kadesh.

7. The Phoenician city of Tyre, from the Gates of Shalmaneser III, 858–825.
8. The city of Parga, Syria, from the Gates of Shalmaneser III, 858–825.
9. The Median city of Kishesim. After the relief from the palace of Sargon II, 722–705, at Khorsabad.

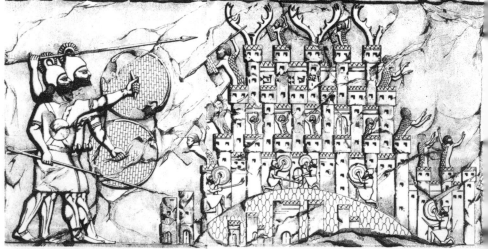

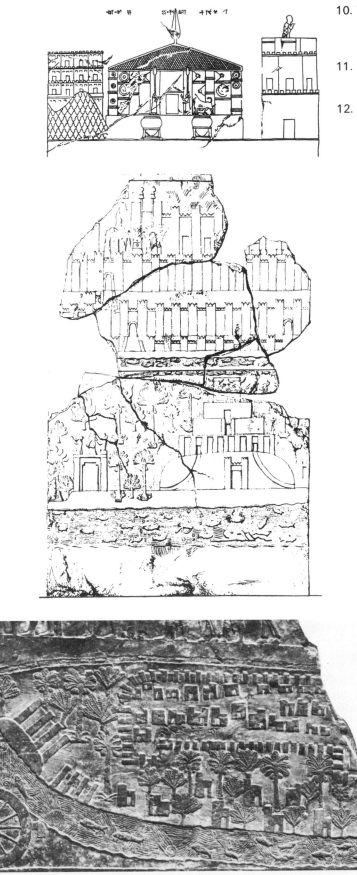

10. The Urartian city of Musasir with the temple of Bagbartu. After the relief from the palace of Sargon II, 722–705, at Khorsabad.
11. The Elamite city of Der. After the relief from the palace of Assurbanipal, 668–627, at Kuyunjik.
12. The Elamite city of Madaktu. Relief from the palace of Assurbanipal, 668–627, at Kuyunjik.

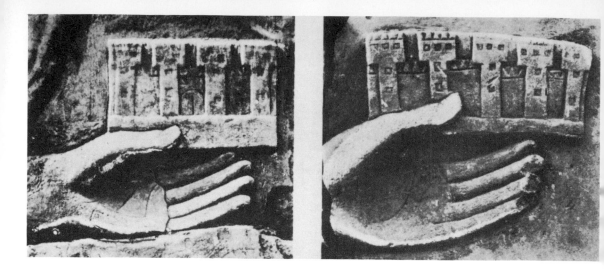

13. City models. Reliefs from the palace of Sargon II, 722–705, at Khorsabad.

14. Fragments of model city, bronze, from Toprakkale, Urartu, 8th century.

15. Rim of vessel with city wall and tower from the Hittite capital, Boghazköy, 18th century.

16. Akkadian map from Nuzi, c. 2500.
17. City plan of Nippur, c. 1500.
18. Fragmentary plan of Babylon, Chaldean period, 6th century.

19. Irrigation channels fed by Euphrates River.
20. Ur (Tell Muqaiyar), city plan.

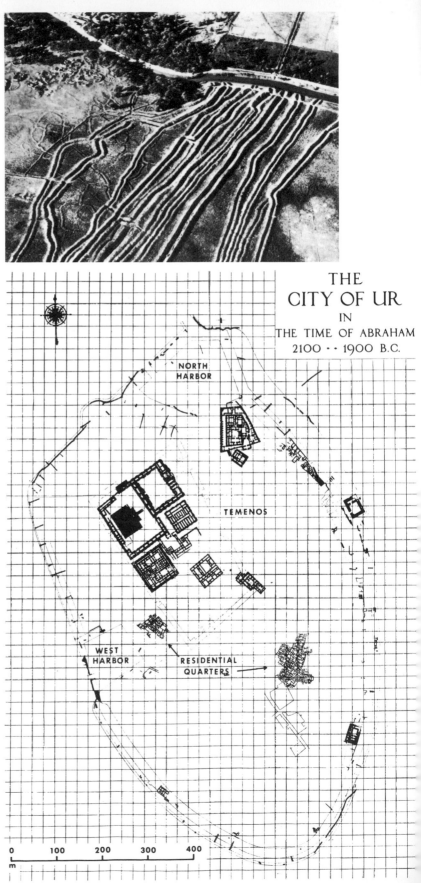

THE
CITY OF UR
IN
THE TIME OF ABRAHAM
2100 · · 1900 B.C.

NORTH
HARBOR

TEMENOS

WEST
HARBOR

RESIDENTIAL
QUARTERS

0   100   200   300   400
m

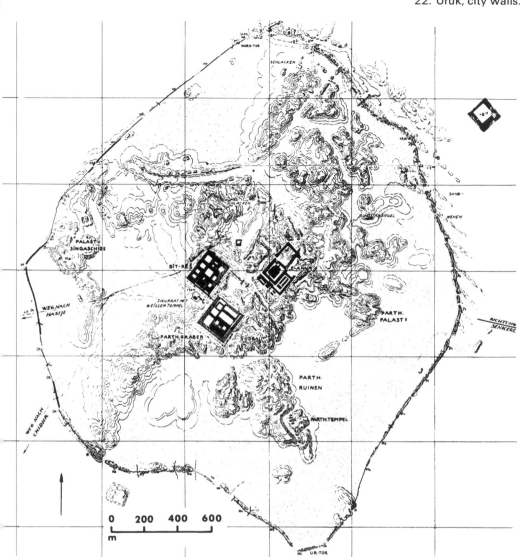

23. Nippur (Niffar), city plan.
24. Eshnunna (Tell Asmar), city plan.

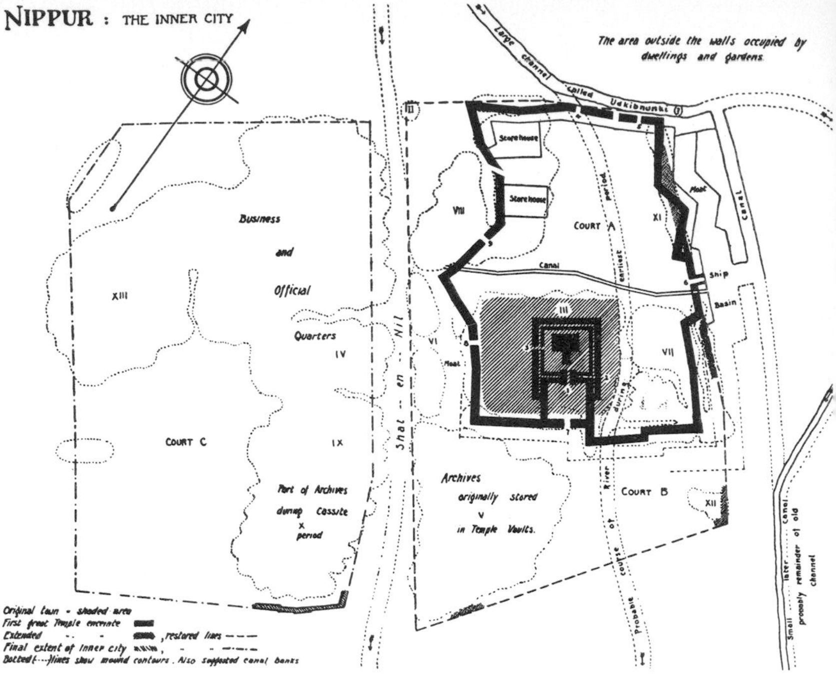

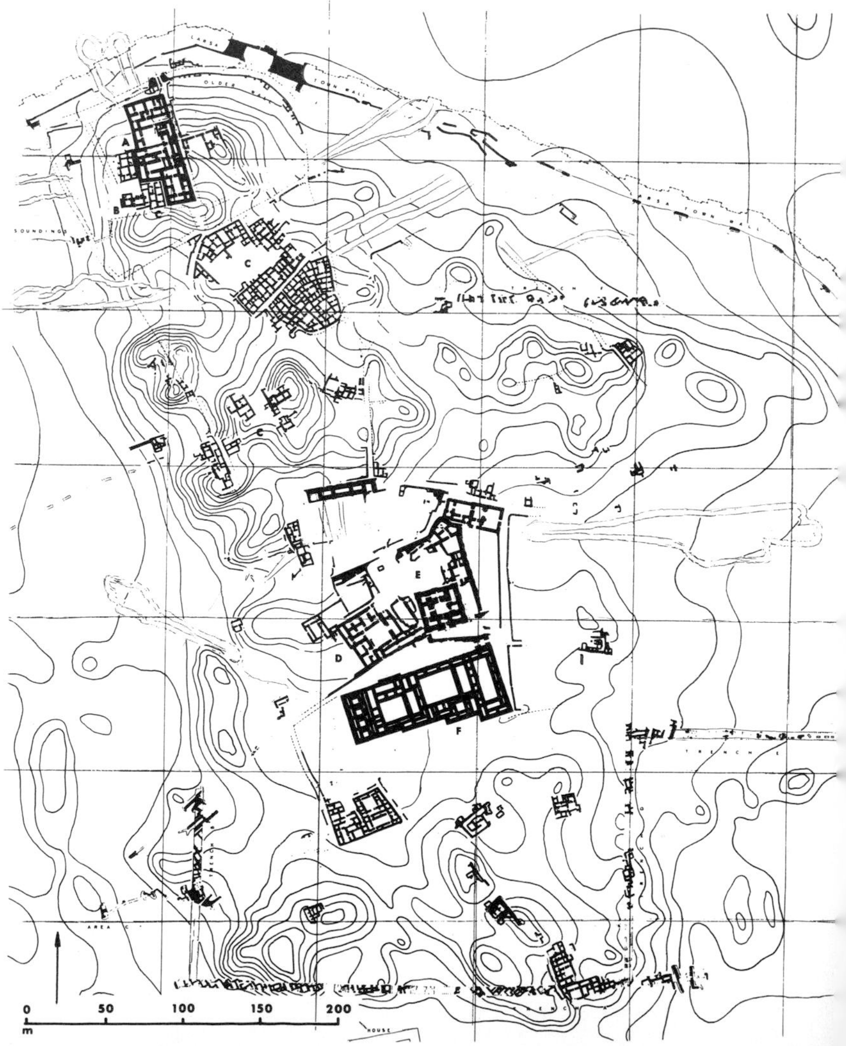

NIPPUR : THE INNER CITY

The area outside the walls occupied by dwellings and gardens.

Business and Official Quarters

Part of Archives dump Cassite period

Archives originally stored in Temple Vaults.

Original town = shaded area
First great Temple enceinte
Citadel , restored lines ----
Final extent of inner city
Dotted lines show mound contours. Also suggested canal banks

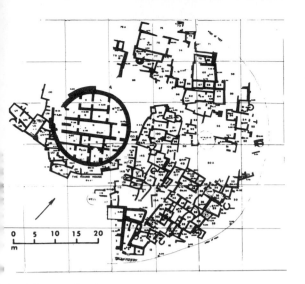

25. Tepe Gawra, Level XI A.
26. Tepe Gawra, Level VI.

27. Nuzi (Yorgan Tepe), excavations. Aerial photo.
28. Assur (Qal'at Sherqat), city plan.

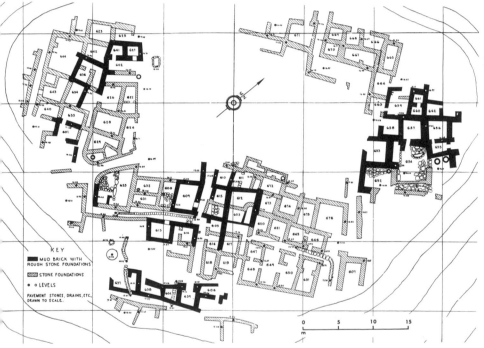

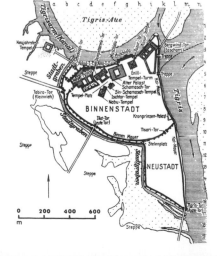

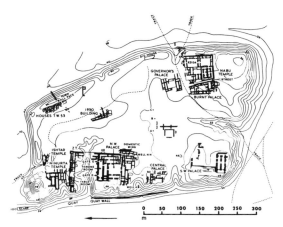

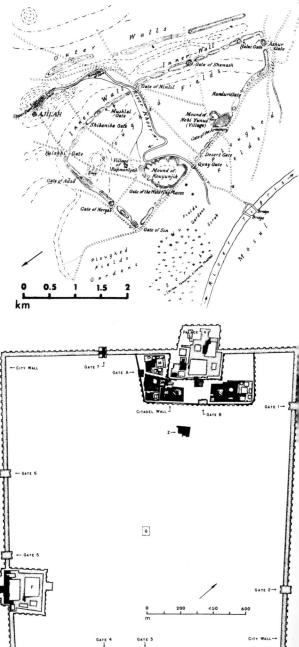

29. Kalhu (Nimrud), aerial photo.

30. Kalhu, Acropolis.

31. Nineveh, plan.

32. Dur Sharrukin (Khorsabad), city plan.

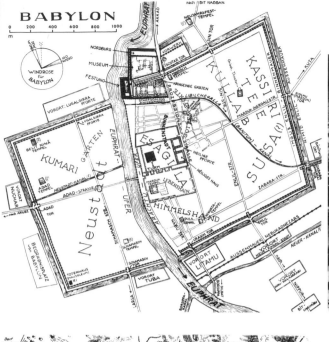

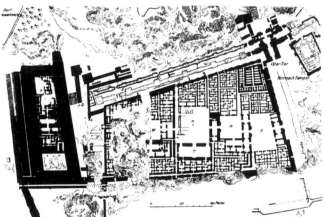

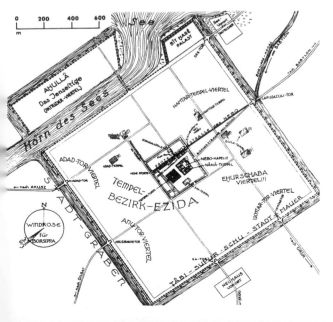

33. Babylon, city plan.
34. Babylon, Esagila and Etemenanki, reconstruction.

35. Babylon, Southern Citadel.
36. Borsippa (Birs Nimrud), city plan.

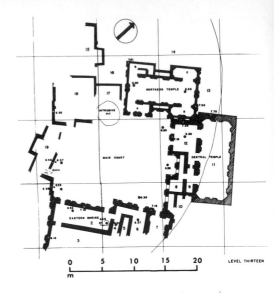

LEVEL THIRTEEN

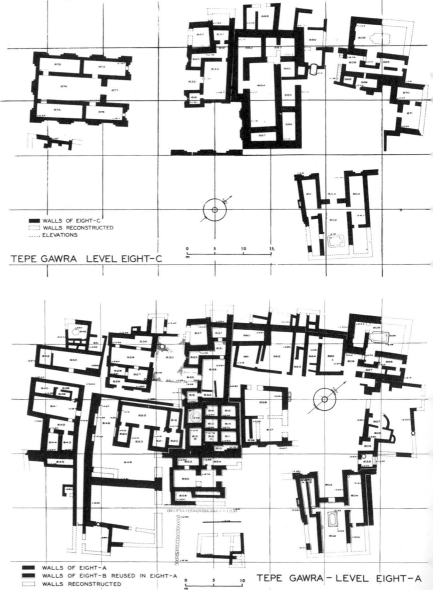

WALLS OF EIGHT-C
WALLS RECONSTRUCTED
ELEVATIONS

TEPE GAWRA LEVEL EIGHT-C

WALLS OF EIGHT-A
WALLS OF EIGHT-B REUSED IN EIGHT-A
WALLS RECONSTRUCTED

TEPE GAWRA - LEVEL EIGHT-A

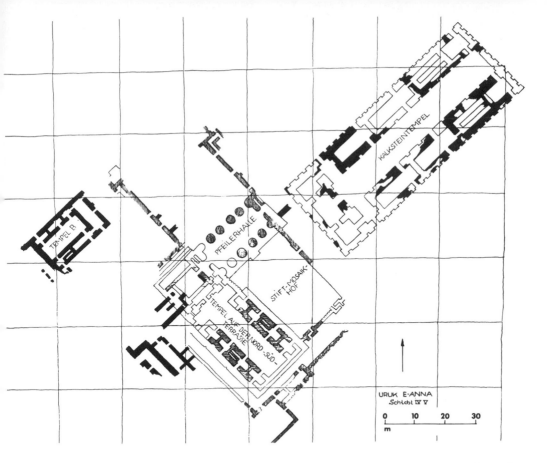

KALKSTEINTEMPEL

TEMPEL B

PFEILERHALLE

STIFT-MOSAIK-HOF

TEMPEL AUF DER NORD-SÜD-TERRASSE

URUK E-ANNA
Schicht IV V

0   10   20   30
m

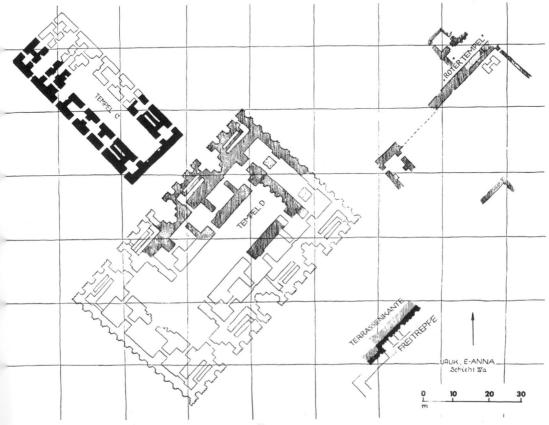

ROTER TEMPEL

TEMPEL C

TEMPEL D

TERRASSENKANTE

FREITREPPE

URUK, E-ANNA
Schicht IVa

0   10   20   30
m

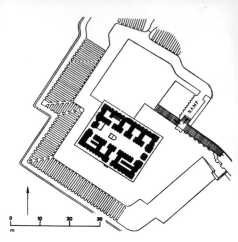

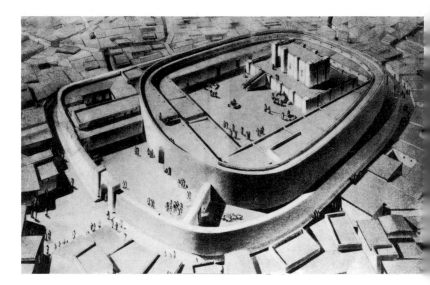

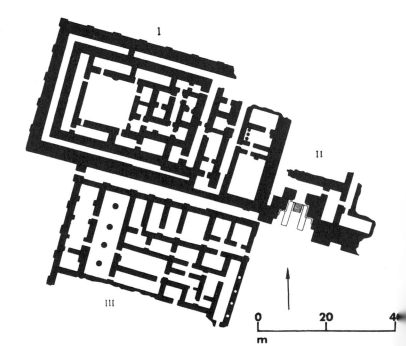

42. Uqair, model of painted temple.

43. Uruk, white temple on its ziggurat.

44. Tutub (Khafajah), temple oval.

45. Kish (Tell Ahaimir), palaces.

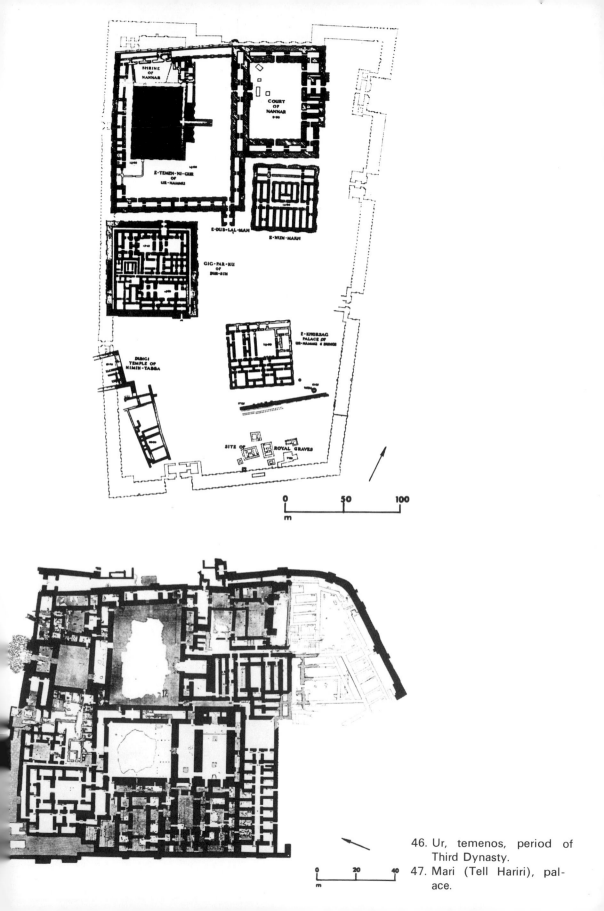

46. Ur, temenos, period of Third Dynasty.

47. Mari (Tell Hariri), palace.

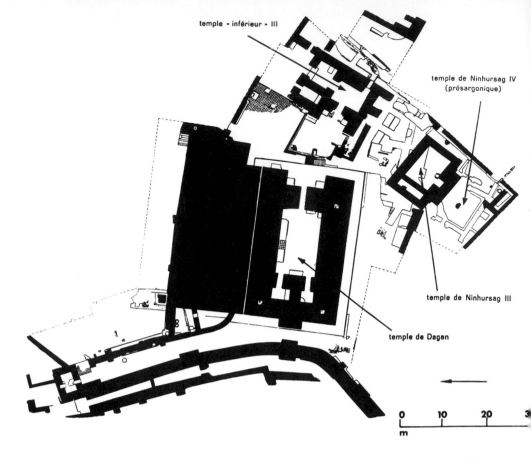

temple · inférieur · III

temple de Ninhursag IV
(présargonique)

temple de Ninhursag III

temple de Dagan

0   10   20   3
m

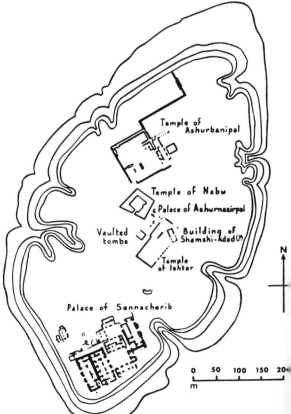

Temple of
Ashurbanipal

Temple of Nabu

Palace of Ashurnazirpal

Vaulted
tombs

Building of
Shamshi-Adad(?)

Temple
of Ishtar

Palace of Sennacherib

N

0   50   100   150   20
m

48. Mari, temples and Assyrian ziggurat.
49. Nineveh, mound of Kuyunjik.

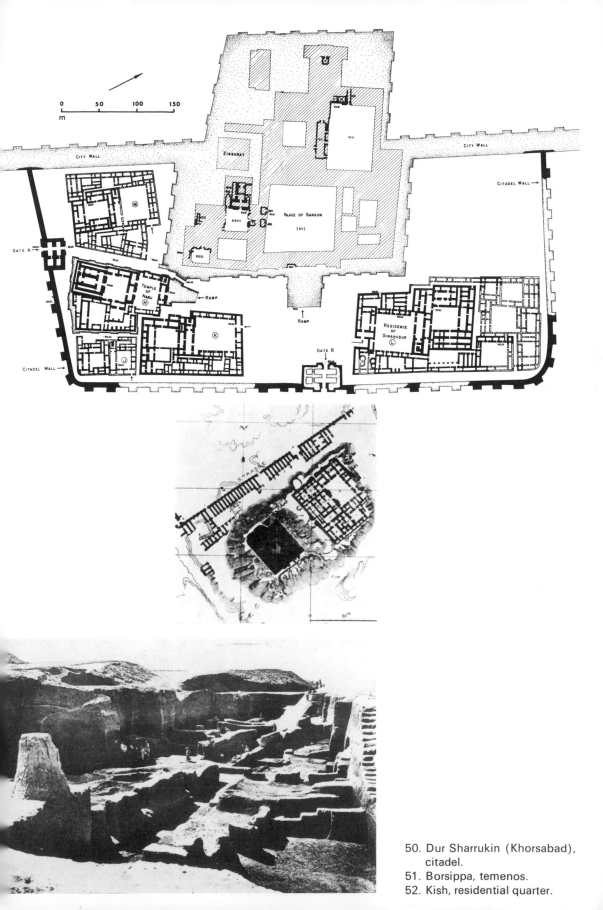

50. Dur Sharrukin (Khorsabad), citadel.
51. Borsippa, temenos.
52. Kish, residential quarter.

53. Mari, residential quarter.
54. Tutub (Khafajah), houses and Sin Temple.

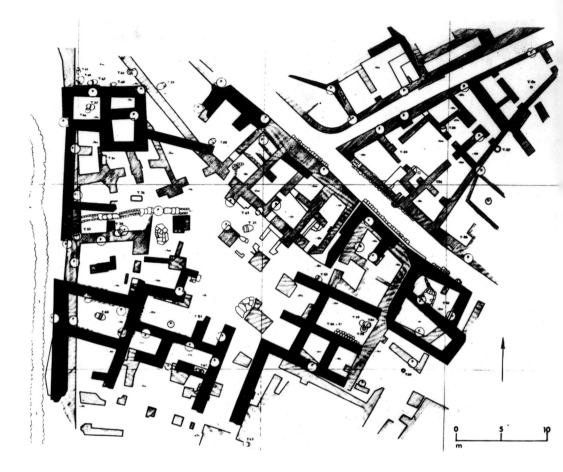

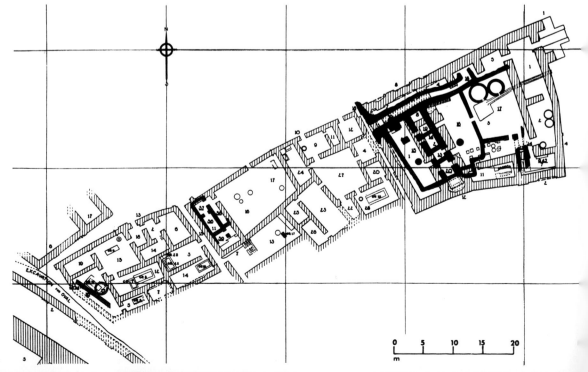

THE
LARSA HOUSES
OF THE E·M SITE

SCALE OF METRES
0   5   10   15   20

55. Ur, residential quarter.
56. Ur, residential quarter.

0   10   20   30
m

57. Assur, residential quarter.
58. Babylon, Merkes Quarter.

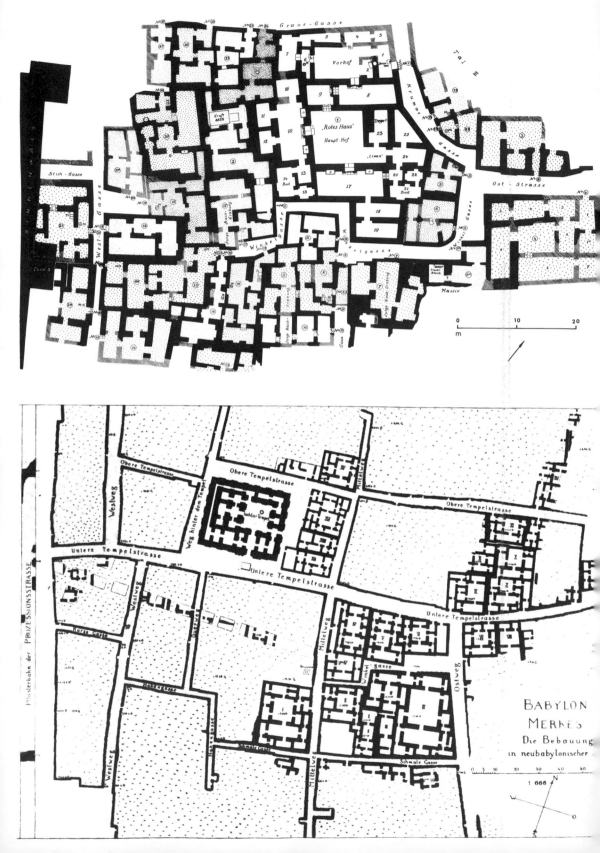

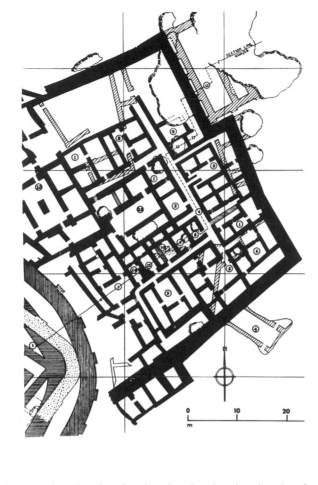

59. Tutub (Khafajah), walled quarter.
60. Shaduppum (Tell Abu-Harmal), city plan.

TELL ABU-HARMAL.

0 10 20 30

61. Slate palette showing fortified cities.

62. Ensign of XXth Nome over sign, "Spat", or district.

63. Signs for "Nut," or town.

64. Memphis, plan of ruins.

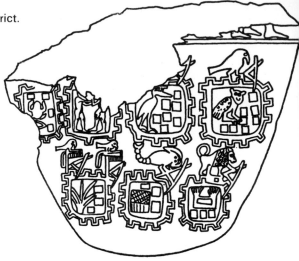

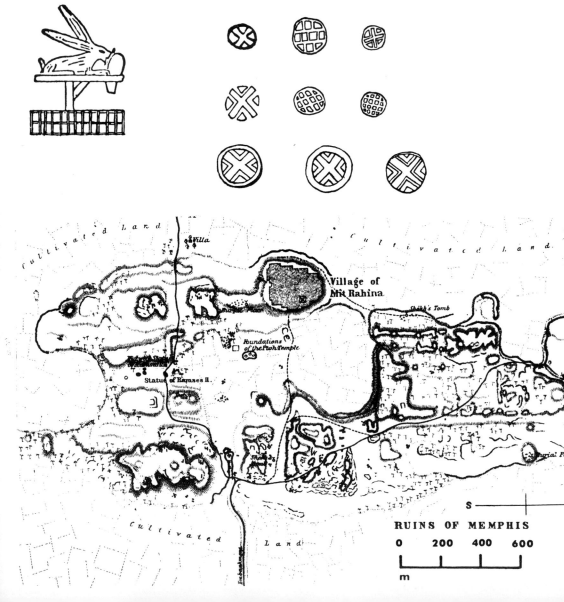

RUINS OF MEMPHIS

0   200   400   600

m

0   50   100   150
m

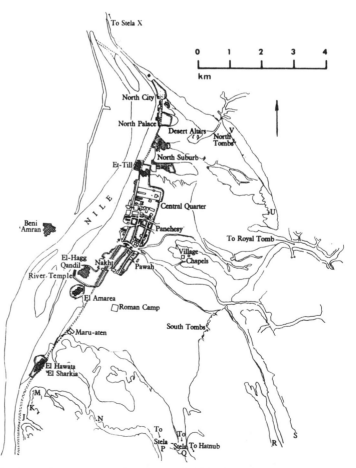

To Stela X

0   1   2   3   4
km

North City
North Palace
Desert Altars
North Tombs
V
North Suburb
Et-Till
Central Quarter
U
Panehesy
To Royal Tomb
Beni 'Amran
Village Chapels
El-Hagg Qandil
Nakht
Pawah
River Temple
El Amarea
Roman Camp
South Tombs
Maru-aten
El Hawata
El Sharkia
NILE
M
K
J
N
To Stela P
To Stela Q
To Hatnub
R
S

67. Thebes, plan of ruins.
68. Opet of Amun (Karnak), plan.

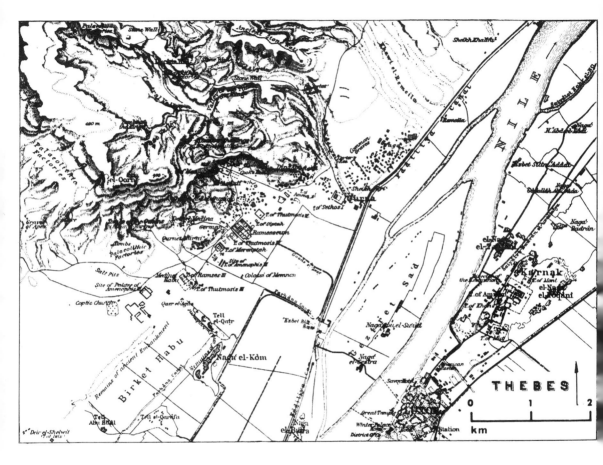

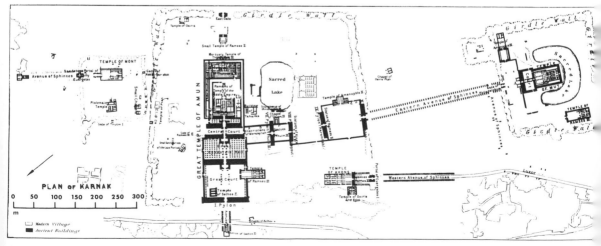

69. Nekhen (Hierakonpolis), plan of town.
70. Nekheb (El Kab), sketch plan of town.
71. El Kab, The Great Walls.

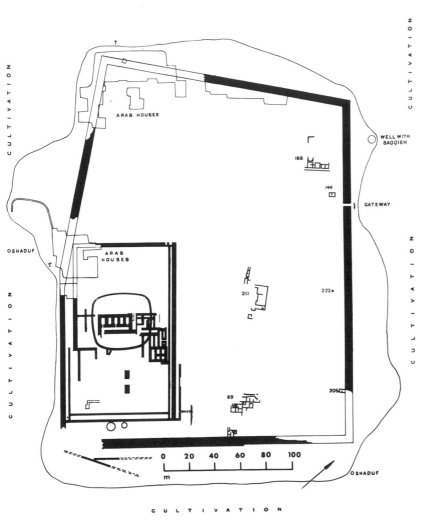

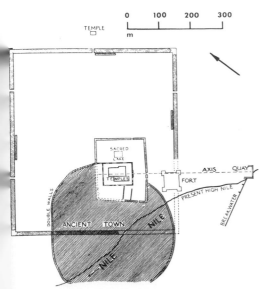

72. Tomb of King Zer, c. 3150, at Abydos.

73. Tomb of King Ka'a, c. 3000, at Abydos.
74. Tomb 3505 at Saqqara.

75. Saqqara, model of pyramid complex of
   King Zoser, c. 2700.

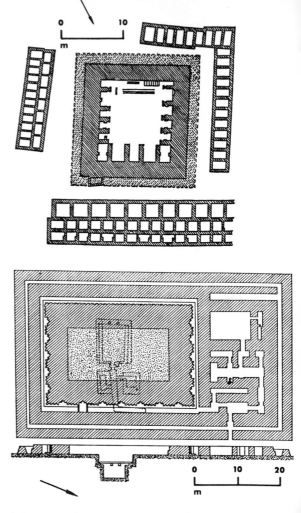

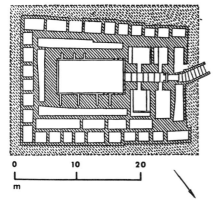

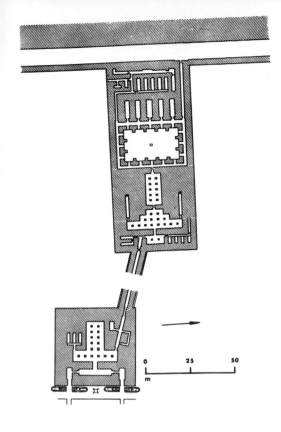

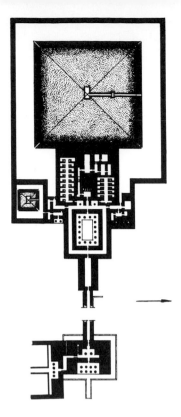

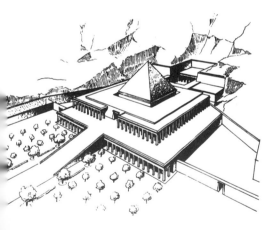

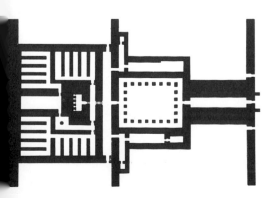

76. Giza, pyramid and valley temples of Chefren.
77. Abusir, pyramid complex of Sahure.

78. Deir el Bahari, mortuary temple of Mentuhotep II.
79. Lisht, pyramid temple of Sesostris I.

80. Giza, aerial photo of pyramids and mastabas from S. W.
81. Giza, pyramid city of Queen Khent-Kawes.

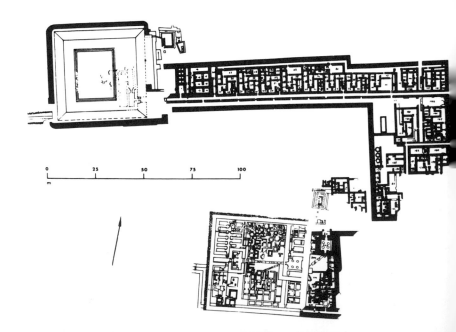

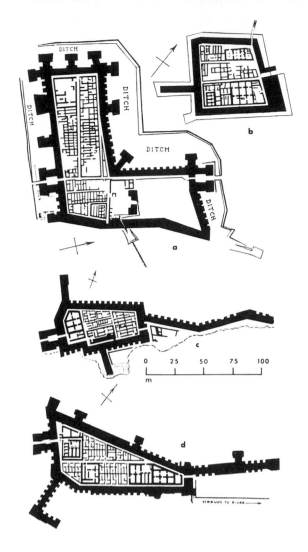

82. a) Fortress city Semne, plan.
    b) Fortress city Kumma, plan.
    c) Fortress city Shalfak, plan.
    d) Fortress city Uronarti, plan.
83. Buhen, fortifications.

84. Sesebi, plan.
85. El Amarna, official central quarter, plan.
86. El Amarna, workmen's
village.

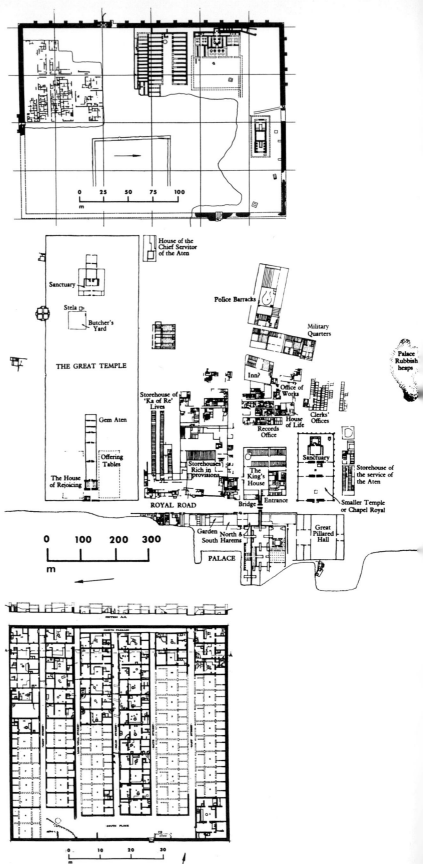

87. El Amarna, main city.
88. Medinet Habu, mortuary
temple of Ramses III.

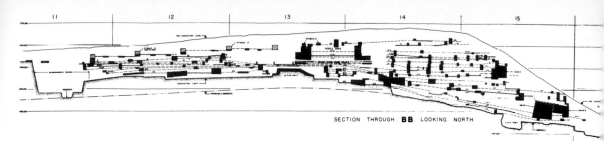

SECTION THROUGH **BB** LOOKING NORTH

89. Megiddo, superimposed city levels.

90. Megiddo, aerial view showing areas of excavation.

91. Alalakh, mound of Atchana, Level IV, V, Palace of Niqmepa at North.

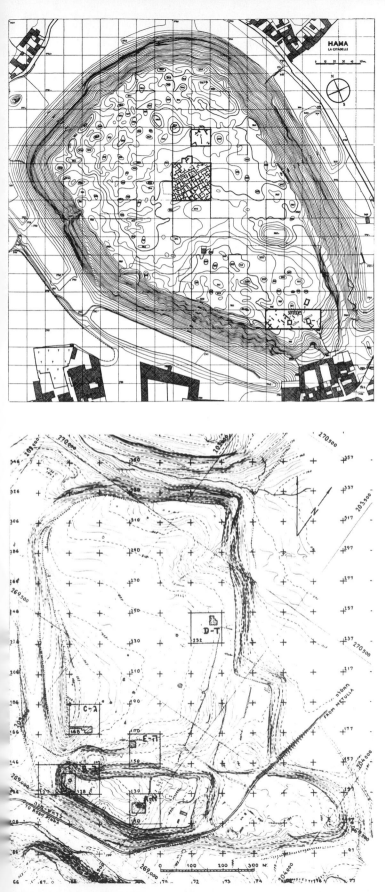

92. Hamath, plan of mound.
93. Hazor, plan, at South—original Tell.

94. Jerusalem, aerial view
with outline of early city.
95. Lachish (Tell ed Duweir),
reconstruction of city of
8th-7th century.

96. Jericho, aerial view of
mound.
97. Ai, the three ramparts of
the lower city.

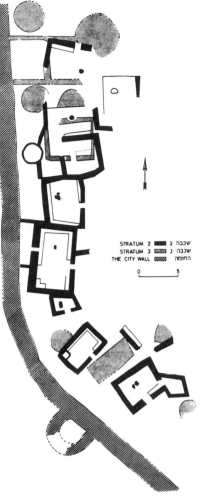

STRATUM 2 ▰ 2 שכבה
STRATUM 3 ▨ ג שכבה
THE CITY WALL ▨ החומה

0   5

98. Arad, city wall and Early Bronze
    Age dwellings.

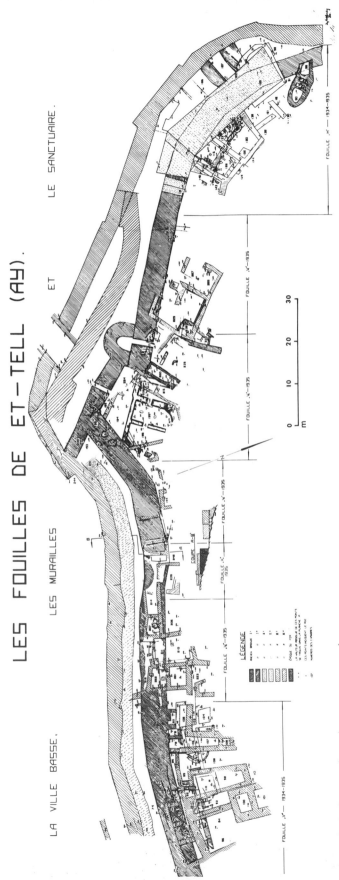

LES FOUILLES DE ET-TELL (AY).

LA VILLE BASSE.

LES MURAILLES.

ET

LE SANCTUAIRE.

99. Ai, Early Bronze Age city, ramparts and sanctuary.

100. Byblos (Gebal), Early Bronze Age fortifications.

101. Megiddo, Early Bronze Age development.
102. Megiddo, terraces and retaining walls, Level XVIII.

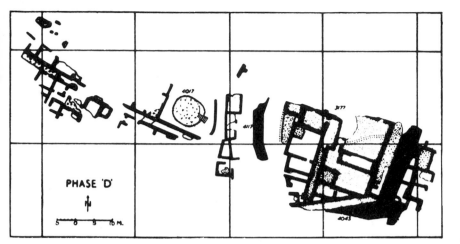

PHASE 'D'

103. Byblos, Early Bronze
     Age levels.
104. Jericho, battered wall
     of late Middle Bronze
     Age.

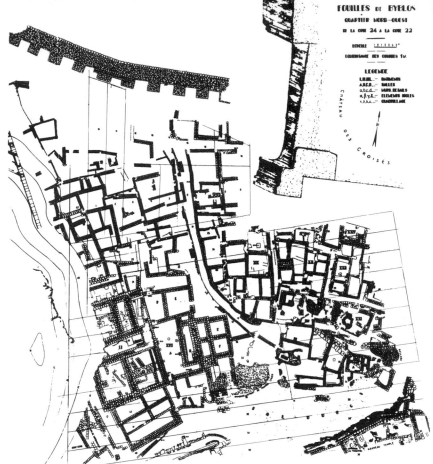

105. Megiddo XIII, reconstructed city gate.
106. Middle Bronze Age city gates.
    a) Gezer
    b) Shechem
    c) Bethshemesh
    d) Alalakh
    e) Qatna
107. Jericho, Middle Bronze Age houses

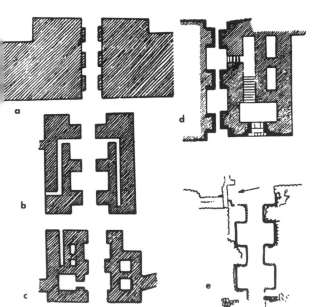

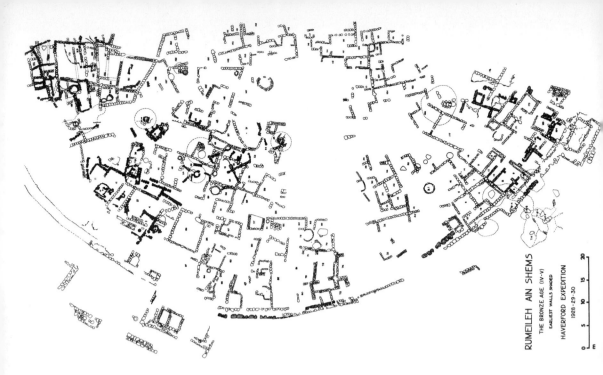

RUMEILEH AIN SHEMS

THE BRONZE AGE (IV-V)
EARLIEST WALLS SHADED
HAVERFORD EXPEDITION
1928-29-30

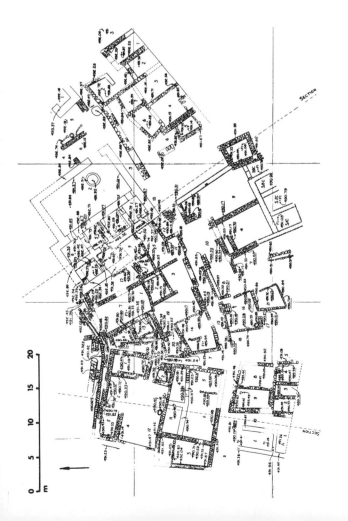

108. Debir (Tell Beit Mirsim), Middle Bronze Age houses.
Section S.E., Stratum D.

109. Bethshemesh (Ain Shems), Middle Bronze-Late Bronze

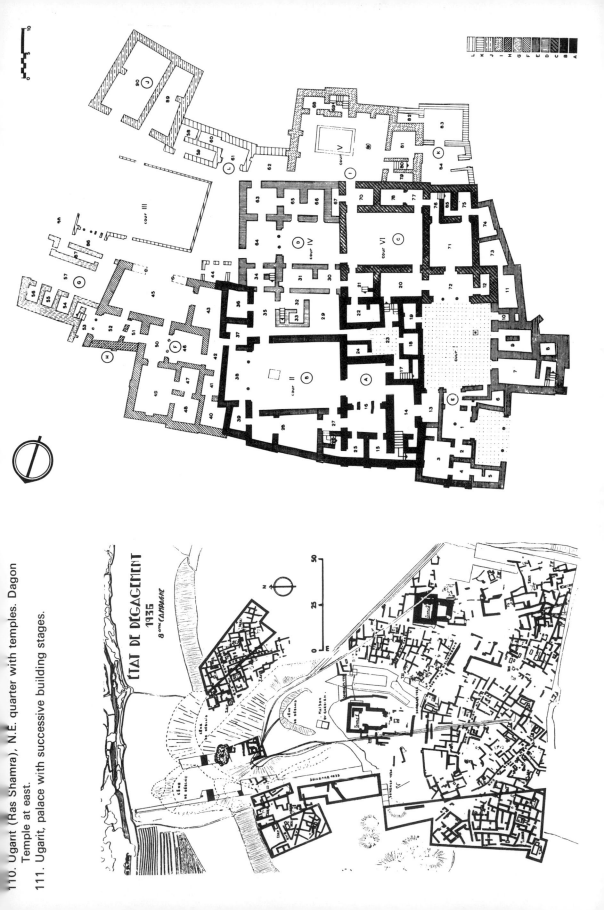

110. Ugarit (Ras Shamra), N.E. quarter with temples. Dagon
Temple at east.

111. Ugarit, palace with successive building stages.

112. Alalakh, residential quarter, Levels 2, 3 at East of tell.
113. Ai, Iron Age city.
114. Tirzah, Level III.

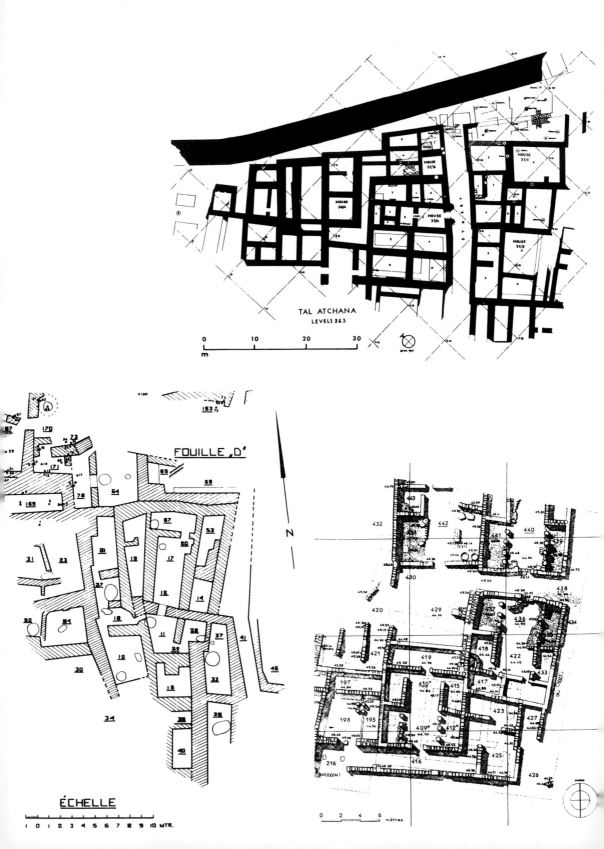

TAL ATCHANA
LEVELS 2&3

0   10   20   30
m

FOUILLE „D'

N

ÉCHELLE

1 0 1 2 3 4 5 6 7 8 9 10 MTR.

0   2   4   6
                    mètres

RUMEILEH - AIN SHEMS

THE IRON AGE (II - III)

LATER WALLS SHADED

HAVERFORD EXPEDITION

1928 - 29 - 30

SCALE

NW   NE

SW   SE

117. Jerusalem, the early city, reconstruction after K. Galling and L. Dressaire.
118. Jerusalem, temple and palace complex.

119. Casement walls and gates.
   a) Megiddo
   b) Gezer
   c) Hazor

120. Samaria, palace complex.

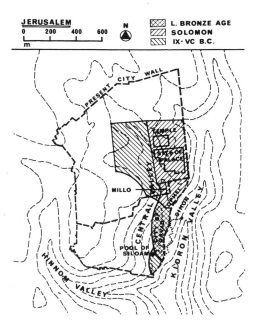

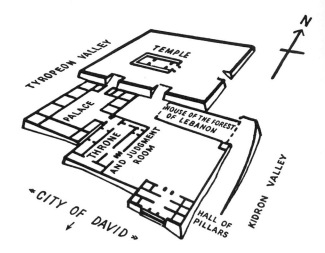

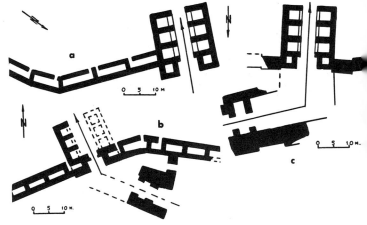

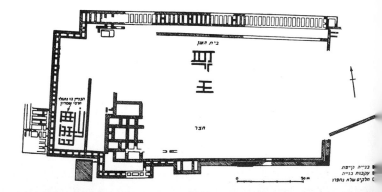

121. Megiddo IV, model of fortified hilltop.
122. Mizpah, fortifications.

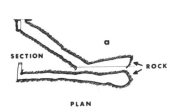

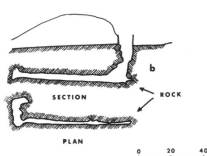

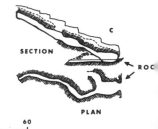

123. Megiddo II, orthogonal layout.
124. Water tunnels.
   a) Gezer
   b) Megiddo
   c) Gibeon
125. Megiddo, water tunnel.

126. Çatal Hüyük, plan of Level VI B, c. 6000.

127. Hacilar, plan of Level II A, c. 5400.

128. Kanesh (Kültepe), plan of mound, I, Karum marked II.

129. Kanesh, Karum, partial excavation.

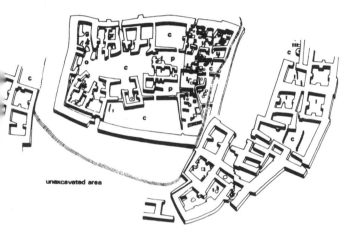

unexcavated area

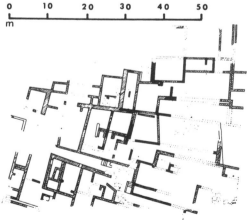

74630

130. Alishar, plan of mound, Level 11T.
131. Hattusas (Bogazköy), city and fortifications.
    Old city at top, citadel at middle, new city at bottom.
132. Büyükkale, the citadel of Hattusas.

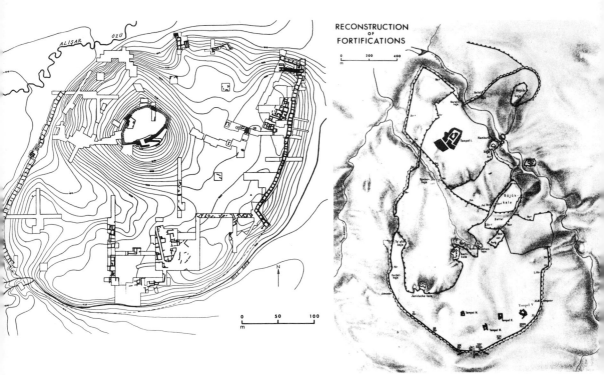

RECONSTRUCTION
OF
FORTIFICATIONS

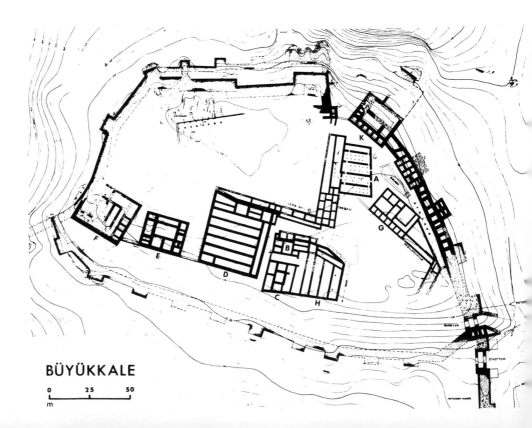

BÜYÜKKALE

133. Hattusas, residential quarter, Level IV.
134. Hattusas, residential quarter of old city, Level II.
135. Hattusas, fortifications.

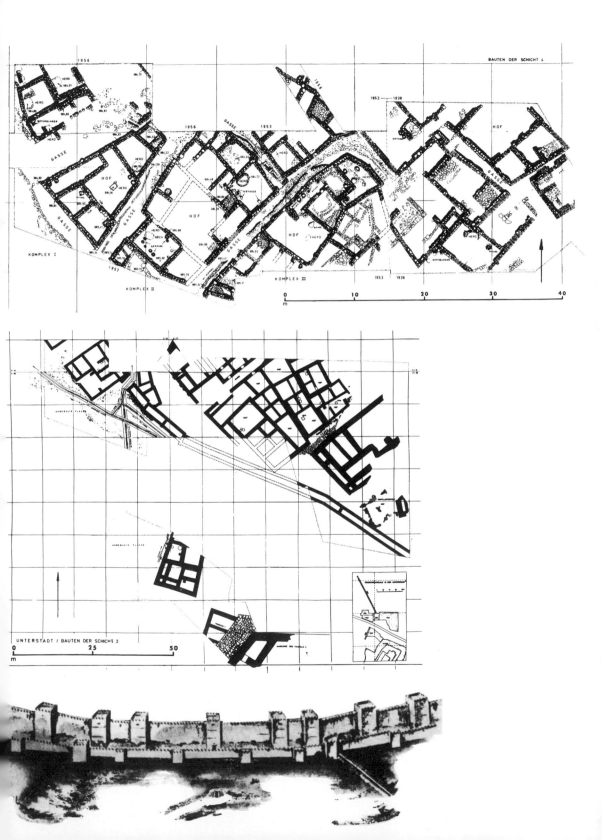

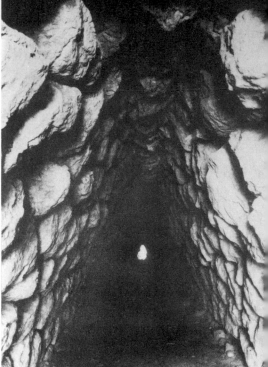

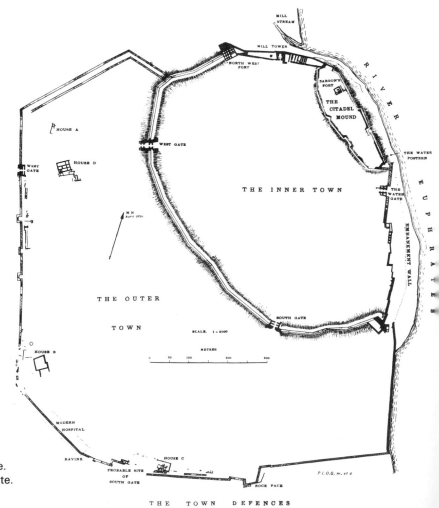

136. Hattusas, Royal Gate.

137. Hattusas, postern gate.

138. Carchemish, plan.

THE TOWN DEFENCES

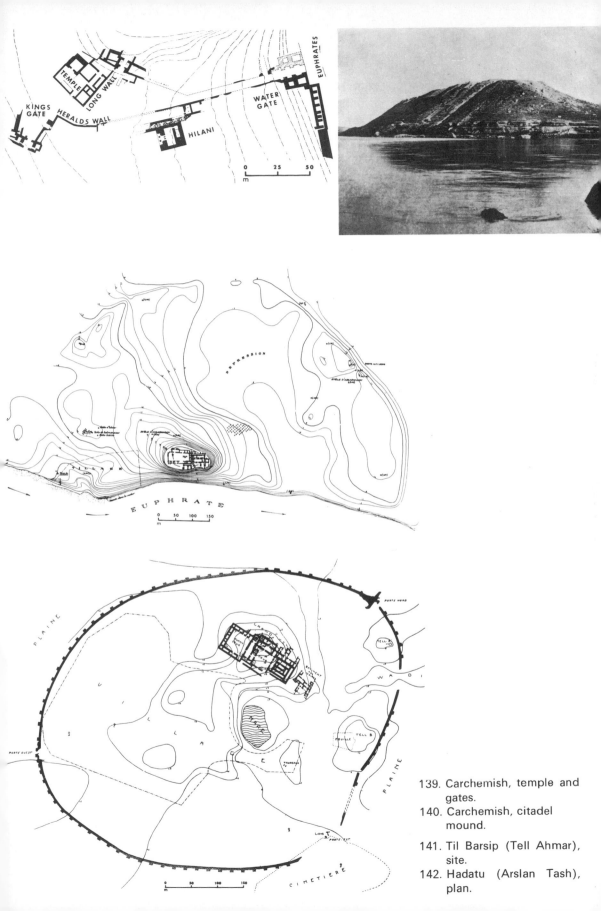

139. Carchemish, temple and gates.
140. Carchemish, citadel mound.
141. Til Barsip (Tell Ahmar), site.
142. Hadatu (Arslan Tash), plan.

143. Guzana (Tell Halaf), plan of city and citadel.
144. Sam'al (Zincirli), plan.

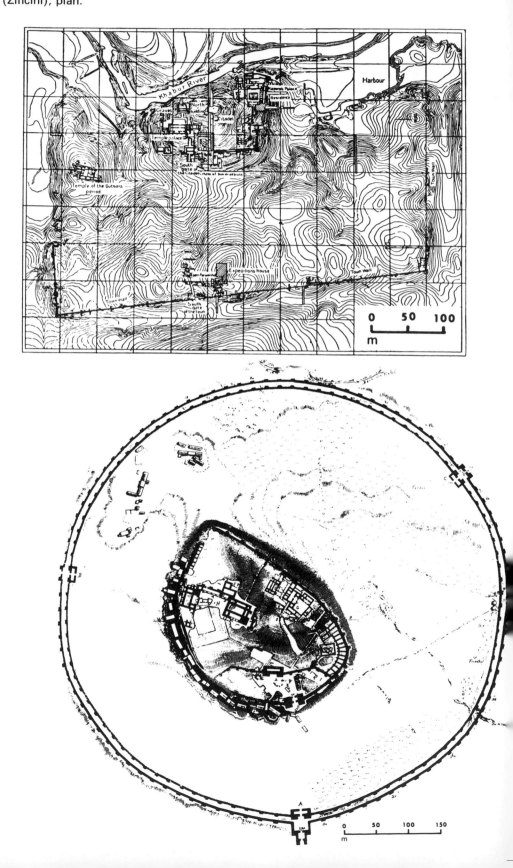

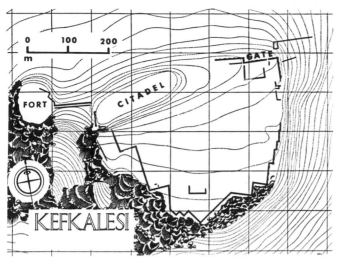

145. Kefkalessi, plan.
146. Tesebaini (Karmir Blur), city
and citadel, 7th century.
147. Tesebaini, citadel.

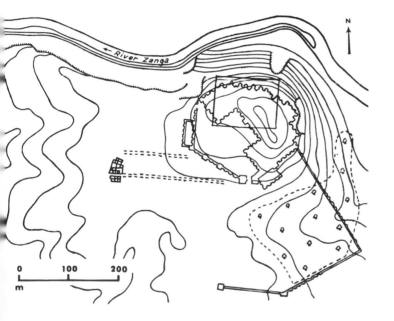

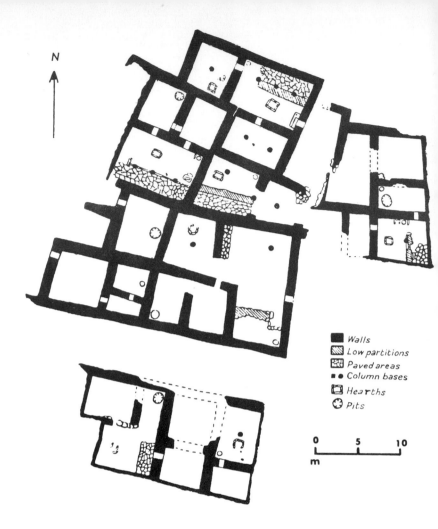

Walls
Low partitions
Paved areas
Column bases
Hearths
Pits

0   5   10
m

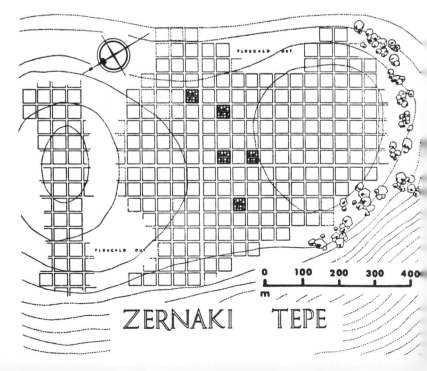

ZERNAKI TEPE

148. Tesebaini, residential
     quarter.
149. Zernaki Tepe, plan.

0   100   200   300   400
m

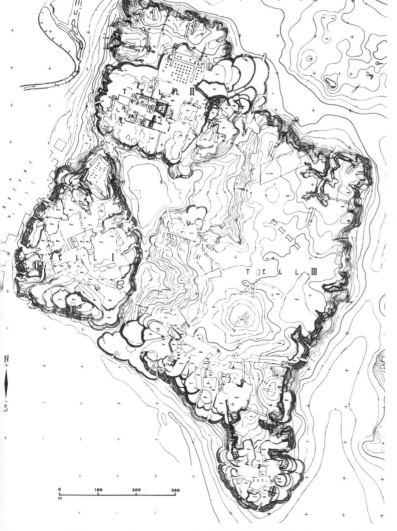

150. Hupshen (Deh-e-Nou), ruin mound.

151. Susa (Shushan-Shush), Plan. Tell I at left, Tell II at top, Tell III at right.

A XII

0   10   20   30
m

152. Susa, Level A XII of Tell III.
153. Dur-Untash (Tchoga Zanbil), 13th century, aerial photo.

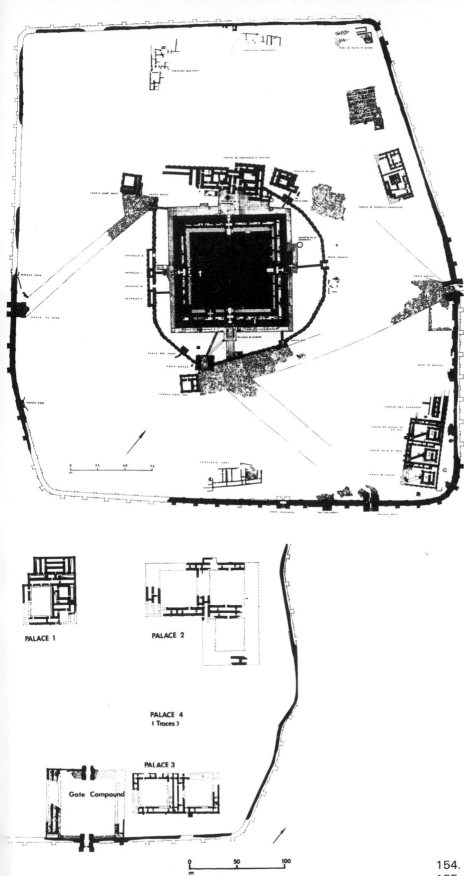

PALACE 1

PALACE 2

PALACE 4
(Traces)

PALACE 3

Gate Compound

154. Dur-Untash, plan.
155. Dur-Untash, palaces.

156. Sialk, reconstruction, beginning of
     First Millennium.
157. Ecbatana (Hangmatana-Hamadan),
     aerial photo.

158. Masjid-i-Suleiman, plan.
159. Masjid-i-Suleiman, terrace.

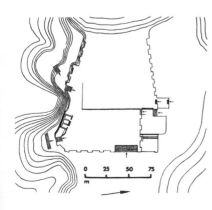

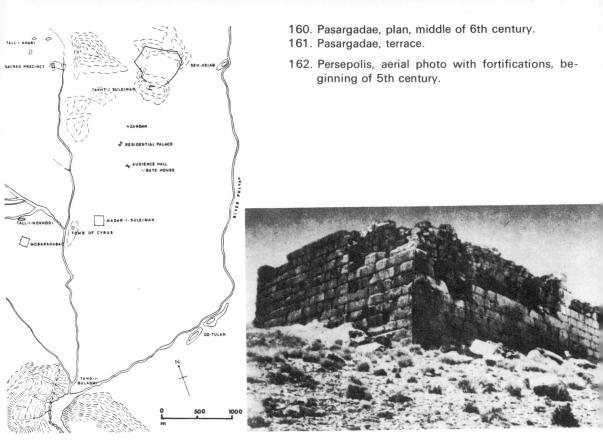

160. Pasargadae, plan, middle of 6th century.
161. Pasargadae, terrace.
162. Persepolis, aerial photo with fortifications, beginning of 5th century.

163. Persepolis, terrace with stairs.
164. Pasargadae, plan of extant buildings.
165. Persepolis, plan.

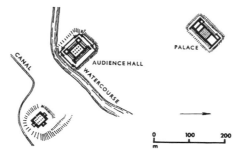

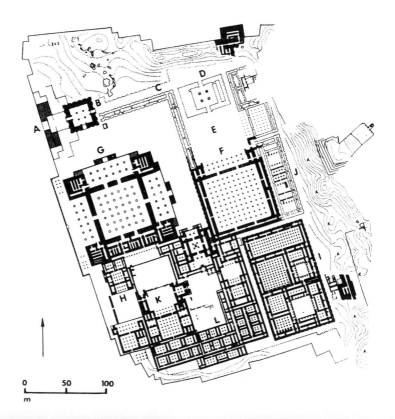

storage of victuals, textiles and utensils; a few larger spaces were employed as wine magazines. Tesebaini covered up to 4 hectares south and west of the citadel, extending along the south edge of the ravine. It was protected on its east and southeast sides by a strong buttressed wall connected to the citadel enclosure. An extension westward beyond a sturdy guard tower was probably planned but never completed. The relatively minor portion of the city that has been excavated shows clusters of up to five dwellings arranged in blocks separated by streets (Fig. 148). Each housing unit is of the same type, with its own entrance, a small open living court, and two rooms.

This standardization of a residential quarter was carried much further in the enigmatic town plan of *Zernaki Tepe* (Fig. 149). This town was planned to occupy the tops of two flat hills overlooking a plain north of Lake Van. It was laid out on a perfect grid, with each identical insula of about 35 square m. accommodating four housing units. The streets were uniformly of 5 m. width except for two main streets, 7 m. wide, intersecting in the center. All houses stood at an equal height of only one course of stone, as the construction of the town was never completed. The date of Zernaki Tepe has been questioned but a comparison of the wall construction makes an Urartian origin quite certain.

The appearance of Urartian cities is suggested by the detailed bronze models found in *Toprakkale* (Fig. 14) and by the relief from the palace of Sargon II in Khorsabad depicting the capture of Musasir (Fig. 10). Multistoried buildings with wooden floors and narrow windows, and flat roofs with parapets and crenelation seem to have been typical.

II. ELAM*

South of the Diyala River the mountain spur of the Pusht-e-Kuh leaves the central Zagros range in a westerly direction and then turns to the southwest separating the Tigris and Euphrates valley from the valleys of the Kerkha and Dez before they all merge north of the Karun River. The plain between Karun and Kerkha (ancient Susiana, today the province of Khuzistan) together with the mountains of Luristan to the north and the Bakhtiari Mountains to the east (ancient Anshan) comprise the heartland of Elam. In the fertile plain where water for irrigation was plentiful, a high urban civilization developed at a very early time similar to that of southern Mesopotamia, often in close cultural contact with it, but just as often in strong competition and a destructive power struggle with it. The mountains of Elam with their riches of minerals, stone, and timber, and the Elamite stud farms, were the envy of the inhabitants of Mesopotamia; throughout history their conquest was the goal of many campaigns.

Kings of *Awan* (a region or city of Elam not yet identified) appear as antagonists of the Early Dynastic kings of Kish and Ur in the Sumerian

*See maps A and B.

king list and are mentioned as adversaries of the kings of Akkad. The kings of *Simash* (the location of which is also unknown) were contemporaries and enemies of the kings of the Third Dynasty of Ur. The devastating raid into Babylonia by Kuter-Nahunte I of Elam in 1711 B.C. and the conquest of Susa by Kurigalzu II of Babylon in the middle of the fourteenth century B.C. exemplify the seesaw conflicts between Elam and Babylonia, as do the later campaigns of Sargon II and Assurbanipal those between Elam and Assyria.

Most of the cities of ancient Elam mentioned in annals and inscriptions, such as *Anshan*, *Awan*, *Adamdun* and *Huhnur*, have not been located; others, such as *Hupshen* (Deh-e-Nou) (Fig. 150) have not been excavated. Only *Susa* and *Dur-Untash* have been explored enough to gain information about Elamite planning practices and the layout of an actual city.

Madaktu, shown in an Assyrian relief (Fig. 12), may suggest the appearance of a typical Elamite city. Located north of Susa, Madaktu was captured by the Assyrians in 655 B.C. shortly before the ultimate destruction of Elamite Susa by Assurbanipal. The relief depicts a scene of the king's triumph. The town is situated between a river and a canal, surrounded by suburbs and palm groves and guarded by two river forts. A strong rampart consisting of alternating towers and curtain walls encloses a town which is summarily depicted by individual houses (probably representing city blocks) separated by not too regular streets.

Susa (Shush), the biblical Shushan, lay in a wide plain on the small river Sha'ur, a tributary of the Dez. It controlled the important roads from Mesopotamia into Iran through the passes of Luristan and the Bakhtiari Mountains. The urban civilization of Susa extends back to the Fourth Millennium B.C. At the time of its conquest by Sargon of Akkad (2334–2279 B.C.) it is mentioned as the capital city of Elam.

Until a few years ago very little was known about Elamite Susa. The enormous multiple city mound (Fig. 151) with occupation levels spanning more than five millennia has been only sporadically investigated, mainly in the northernmost Tell II, the upper layers of which contained the ruins of the Achaemenid Palace and the Apadana of Artaxerxes II (404–360 B.C.) probably built on top of earlier, leveled Elamite royal dwellings. Tell I, the "Acropolis" where Darius erected a citadel in c. 500 B.C., is formed by the earliest prehistoric settlements and was the old Elamite "Upper City"—without doubt the site of the holy precinct with the ziggurat and temple of Inshushinak that was crowned by the famous bronze "Horns" taken as spoils by Assurbanipal in the seventh century. It is now being excavated. Tell III, which the excavators call the "Royal City," was the Elamite "Lower City," total surface 55.8 hectares, consisting of residential and commercial quarters. It has now been explored in a limited part of a city quarter dating back to the middle of the Second Millennium B.C.

Level XIIA of this area (Fig. 152) shows a section of a strong buttressed wall, in all likelihood the enclosure of a sanctuary; farther north was found a large, free-standing rectangular house with two open courts. Nearby are the irregular configurations of two blocks of commercial buildings and two blocks of schools. The eastern corner is taken up by a vast palace-like townhouse built around a number of open courtyards. No coherent town plan or principle of orientation is recognizable; rather, we see a development of uncontrolled growth emanating from the single house unit. The limits of growth were set by established thoroughfares and available space. There is as little regard for the relationship between open and built-up areas as in the development of Mesopotamian cities discussed earlier.

Dur-Untash (Tchoga Zanbil)

> Having supplied the building material I built here Dur-Untash and the Holy Precinct. With an inner and outer rampart I enclosed it. A ziggurat, unlike anything former kings had made, I erected and dedicated it to the gods Humban and Inshushinak, the guardians of the Holy Precinct. What I have built and wrought be devoted to them. May the grace and justice of Humban and Inshushinak rule this place.
>
> Hinz, *Elam*, 96

Thus Untash-Gal, King of Elam from 1275 to 1240 B.C., consecrated one of the most grandiose town planning schemes conceived in the ancient world. A large plateau about 30 km. southeast of Susa, rising between the Dez and Sha'ur River valleys and protected in the northeast by a mountain range, was chosen as the site for the "Holy City" of Dur-Untash (Fig. 153).

Planning on a gigantic scale preceded the actual construction. Millions of sun-dried and baked bricks were prefabricated near the bed of the Dez, where water and firewood were plentiful, and were brought by mule and donkey caravans to the building site 1.5 km. away. As the water on the plateau was brackish and the site was 60 m. above the level of the Dez, Untash-Gal decided to bring the water of the Kerkha, famous for its good quality, by means of a canal over 50 km. long to a huge reservoir outside the city and thence to a communicating basin inside the walls.

These outer ramparts more than 4000 m. in circumference, probably planned as a rectangle concentric to the temenos inside, were modified to exploit the topographical features of the site, particularly in the south where the walls merge in a great arc and in the northeast where the walls open outward, designed in all likelihood to give ultimately a protected access to the Dez River.

The Royal Quarter, with its own fortified gate, was located in the eastern section of the city; the residential and commercial districts of the city that were planned for a zone between the inner and outer ramparts were never built. Apparently all work ceased with the death of Untash-Gal (1240 B.C.) after only the temenos, the palaces, and the city walls

115

had been completed. The large holy precinct (Fig. 154), a slightly irregular rectangle of about 350 m. by 450 m., was enclosed by a strong
wall, similar to the outer ramparts. This wall, with its alternating buttresses
and pilasters, was entered through three unevenly spaced gates. The
temenos contained a number of temples dedicated to various deities of
the vast Elamite pantheon. It was dominated by the ziggurat with its own
enclosure wall of irregular oval shape, provided with seven gates.

The excavation plans of Dur-Untash, though not complete, are highly
revealing with regard to Elamite planning. Temple tower, temenos, and
city followed the principle of corner orientation. It was obvious that
they were integrally conceived and correlated. But the clear geometry of
the ziggurat complex was not carried into the design of the enclosure
walls or of the surrounding temple compounds, which, though mostly
rectangular, lack uniform orientation and show no evidence of being
part of an over-all plan. These various structures are placed in the open
grounds within the temenos like so many self-contained pavilions. It is
not unlikely that the unpaved areas were planted, or were meant to be
planted, with a sacred grove which, according to literary sources, was
an indispensable feature of an Elamite temple precinct.

An interesting principle of Elamite planning apparent in the temenos
plan is the "diagonal approach" which establishes a distinct relationship
between the gates of the outer and inner walls and must have had
religious and possibly esthetic significance. On a smaller scale this
diagonal approach also underlies the plan of the subsidiary temples.

Remnants of a temporary residential quarter were excavated within
the holy precinct near its outer northwestern wall. The buildings were
flimsily built and of irregular configuration.

The Royal Quarter is only partially preserved (Fig. 155). Three existing palaces and traces of a fourth have been found. All these buildings
seem to have been erected as separate entities without any general
compositional relationships. They were situated within a garden or
park and oriented to face the prevailing breeze.

Common to all palaces and the gate compound is a peculiar arrangement (apparently typically Elamite) of single, double and triple rows of
rooms of equal width grouped around interior courtyards.

III. IRAN*

Like gigantic ramparts linked by a huge corner bastion, the Elburz
range and the Zagros chain extend east and southeastward from the
towering mountain massif of Armenia to enclose the Iranian highland
and join up with the wall-like mountain chains of Central Asia in the
east. Through the few natural gateways penetrating these mountain
barriers in the north there passed a host of tribes and peoples of various
racial backgrounds from the inexhaustible human reservoir of the Asiatic

*See map A.

116

steppes. These hordes sought to settle in Iran or to cross the mountain passes in the west to reach the attractive regions of the "Fertile Crescent" and Anatolia.

While Central Iran, with its arid wastes and salt deserts, could not support life, the numerous valleys of the great surrounding mountain chains, particularly in the north and west, offered, depending on altitude, rainfall and fertility, good pasturage for goats, sheep, and horses, and the conditions for the cultivation of grapes, other fruits, and grain. A glance at the map shows that both the early and later settlement follow the great arc of the mountain ranges, as do the major caravan and trade routes.

Sialk

While prehistoric settlements in Iran have been traced back as far as the Fifth and even the Sixth Millennium B.C., the earliest town explored to date hails only from the beginning of the First Millennium B.C. A fortified town and citadel (Fig. 156) built on the southern hill of Sialk by a powerful chieftain of the newly arrived Aryan tribesmen is probably typical of the feudal strongholds designed to keep the local population in check.

Ecbatana

According to Herodotus, *Ecbatana* (Hangmatana or "Place of Assembly") was built by Deioces, the legendary first king of the Medes (probably Daiokku, the Median Chieftain defeated by Sargon II in 715 B.C.) to serve as fortified capital and residence city for the control of the towns and domains of his feudal vassals. The city as described by Herodotus was surrounded by seven tiers of strong fortification walls which rose one above the other, following the contours of the hill, and was crowned by the palace of the king. *Kishesim* (Fig. 9), a town in northwestern Iran taken by Sargon II and depicted on a relief in his palace at Khorsabad, provides a fitting illustration for this description of Ecbatana and shows what might have been a typical fortified Median town.

Ecbatana controlled the main east-west and north-south routes of Northern Iran and lay athwart the road leading from Mesopotamia through the gap of Bisutun to the Iranian plateau. Because of its strategic location and the pleasant climate afforded by its high altitude, it served as northern capital and summer residence for the kings of the Achaemenid Empire.

Today, the oval city mound of ancient Ecbatana, still recognizable within the built-up area of Hamadan (Fig. 157), remains unexcavated. So too is a second, largely unoccupied mound which was probably the site of the Achaemenid palace.

Achaemenid "Cities"

No substantial remains of cities from the Achaemenid period have yet been discovered, and it is unlikely that any will be found in the future, except perhaps of those cities which were conquered and taken over by the Persians, such as Ecbatana, Susa, or Babylon. It seems that the Achaemenids did not build cities in the true sense.

Meager remnants of mud-brick and wood houses, dating from the Achaemenid period, may be seen near *Istakhr* at the foot of the platform of *Persepolis*, widely dispersed over the plain of *Pasargadae* and around the terrace of *Masjid i Suleiman;* these suggest that they had the character of shantytowns, supplementing the tent cities surrounding the temporary royal residences, where most of the officials, priests, soldiers and retainers lived during the king's visits.

The glory, power and wealth of the Achaemenid Great Kings found tangible expression in ceremonial palaces. It was to their construction and decoration that the kings directed their main architectural and artistic ambitions. Three design elements in the repertory of the Achaemenid architects stand out as chief contributions to monumental planning: The elevated terrace, the open monumental stair and the free-standing hypostyle (pillared) hall.

The imposing artificial terraces at Masjid-i-Suleiman (Fig. 158, 159) and Bard-i-Nishandah, not far from the Karun River, were built of large stone blocks against the mountainside, and were reached by a series of monumental stairs. The terraces are thought to have supported the residences and subsidiary buildings of the first Achaemenid tribal chieftains.

At Pasargadae, the "Camp of the Persians" (Fig. 160), the high platform of Takht-i-Suleiman (Fig. 161), dating back to Cyrus (559–530 B.C.), is part of a fortification system which encloses a valley between two hills to its north.

The most grandiose terrace of all was constructed at Persepolis (Fig. 162) against the slope of the "Kuh-i-Rahmat," the "Mount of Mercy," which served thus as an extension of its fortification system. Built of tightly fitted ashlars of irregular shape, it rose up to 20 m. above the plain, and its surface measured not less than 13 hectares. The open "Grand Staircases" of Persepolis (Fig. 163) were unmatched in the history of architectural composition until the Baroque period, more than two thousand years later. The roots of this monumental stone architecture may be found in Urartian constructions which, however, did not advance beyond the stage of "civil engineering."

Neither Pasargadae nor Persepolis have the appearance of permanent "capitals," and they could not have functioned as such. Both lack permanent residence palaces with necessary dependencies, administration buildings and service quarters. Persepolis was a ceremonial center where, once a year, the high officials and dignitaries of the Empire gathered at the New Year's celebration to pay homage and tribute to the "King of Kings." Except for the barracks that housed the permanent garrison and the vaultlike treasury, all building was audience, reception, and banqueting halls for ceremonial purposes. Only temporary residence facilities were provided for the king and his entourage.

Cyrus the Great's new "residence" at Pasargadae must have served the special purpose of providing a religious and political center in the heartland of "Parsa" (today, Fars) where probably the royal treasure was kept in the fortified precinct mentioned.

The ruins of only three substantial buildings (Fig. 164) remain of Cyrus' palace compound on the Pulvar Plain. A monumental gatehouse gave entry through an enclosure wall into parklike grounds containing water channels and a basin. Here, separate, informally arranged pavilions housed the various functions of the royal court. Two large, freestanding hypostyle structures served as audience-and-reception rather than residence hall.

At Persepolis, where space was more confined, the building complex still consisted essentially of individual, closely juxtaposed pavilions of vast dimensions (Fig. 165). It appears doubtful that an over-all layout was worked out before the construction of the separate units began. The single buildings such as the "Apadana" (G) or the "Tachara" (H) of Darius or of Xerxes (K) were strictly symmetrical or balanced in plan, and the treasury complex (I) and the guest wing (L) were clearly organized in their layout. Similarly, the axial relationship of the terrace's "Grand Staircase" (A) to the "Gate of All Lands" (B) and to the processional street (C), and of the unfinished gatehouse (D) to the parade ground (E) and Throne Hall (F) were carefully established. However, there was an inexplicable lack of coaxiality between the gate of Xerxes (B) and the Apadana (G), and a complete absence of compositional relationship between the banqueting halls of Darius (H) and Xerxes (K) and the Apadana (G), or of the Treasury (I) to the Throne Room-Barracks complex (F-J). There is, however, a uniform northwest-southeast orientation of all buildings in keeping with the main axis of the platform.

It seems that the Persians did not develop integrally conceived, coherent, completely organized, large-scale planning schemes before the Seleucid and Sassanian periods, when they came under Hellenistic and Roman influence, respectively.

While the Achaemenid kings apparently did not, as already stressed, build new cities, they were active in the reconstruction and modernization of the existing and adopted capitals of the empire. Susa, for example, has yielded evidence of the ambitious urban renewal efforts of Darius the Great, although so far no judgment about the layout of his rebuilt city and the character of its residential quarters are possible. Darius not only built his new palace and citadel, but completely restored the city wall and surrounded it by a moat fed by the Sha'ur River, virtually turning Susa into an island fortress.

Too little is known to date to make a general statement about the planning philosophy of the ancient peoples in the area known as modern Persia and Armenia. They expended tremendous physical effort to produce monumental secular and religious structures. But no integral over-all planning scheme resulted. The cruciform grid plan of the Urartian city of Zernaki Tepe (Fig. 149) is unique and at present inexplicable.

POSTSCRIPT

A Neo-Babylonian clay tablet in the British Museum shows an ideal map of the ancient world with the city of Babylon located in the center of the cosmos. Literary sources allude to celestial prototypes of Mesopotamian cities. But, surprisingly, no evidence has been found yet in the ancient Near East, unlike the Far East, of a city plan based on cosmic symbolism. Ezekiel's vision of the City of God (Ez 48:30) implies such a concept, but it remains merely that—a utopian vision.

The conquest of Alexander the Great (337–323 B.C.) changed the face of the ancient Near East: a single, foreign civilization was superimposed upon its old diverse cultures. New principles were applied to the planning of cities and monumental buildings, but they did not reach beyond the old ones. Behind the great new colonnades, the grand facades, the splendid temple complexes, and the civic centers, the indigenous ancient cities hardly changed their character. The residential quarters continue their own informal organic life of growth and decay without much interference, so that today many Near Eastern cities off the main thoroughfares have very much the same aspect as a few thousand years ago.

SELECTIVE BIBLIOGRAPHY

This bibliography takes the place of notes which, in order to be exhaustive, would be too numerous. Literature on individual sites may be found in the bibliographies of volumes given here.

Key to Abbreviations

ANET Ancient Near Eastern Texts Relating to the Old Testament (J. B. Pritchard)

BASOR Bulletin of the American Schools of Oriental Research, New Haven

IEJ Israel Exploration Journal, Jerusalem

MMAS Metropolitan Museum of Art Studies, New York

TPR Town Planning Review, Liverpool

GENERAL

Adams, R. M., "The Origin of Cities." *Scientific American*, Vol. 203, No. 3 (Sept. 1960).

Andrae, W., *Alte Feststrassen im Nahen Osten*. Stuttgart, 1964.

Badawy, A., *Architecture in Ancient Egypt and the Near East*. Cambridge, 1966.

Childe, G., "The Urban Revolution." *TPR*, XXI (1950).

Egli, E., *Geschichte des Städtebaues I, Die alte Welt*. Zürich, 1959.

Frankfort, H., *The Art and Architecture of the Ancient Orient*. Baltimore, 1954.

———*The Birth of Civilization in the Near East*. New York, 1956.

Kraeling, C. H., and Adams, R. M., ed. *City Invincible, A Symposium on Urbanization and Cultural Development in the Ancient Near East*. Orient. Inst., U. of Chicago, 1960.

Lavedan, P., *Histoire de l'urbanisme I*. Paris, 1926.

———*Géographie des villes*. Paris, 1936.

Mumford, L., *The City in History*. New York, 1961.

National Geographic Magazine, *Everyday Life in Ancient Times*. Washington, 1951.

Pirenne, J., *La ville. Recueils de la société J. Bodin VI-VIII*. Brussels, 1954.

Schmidt, J., "Strassen in altorientalischen Wohngebieten." *Baghdader Mitteilungen*, III, Berlin, 1964.

Woolley, C. L., *The Beginning of Civilization*. New York, 1965.

Yadin, Y., *The Art of Warfare in Biblical Lands*. New York, 1963.

IDEA AND IMAGE

Bible, The, King James Version; New World Translation; Author's Translation.

Botta, P. E., and Flandin, E., *Monument de Ninive*. Paris, 1849–1850.

Breasted, J. H., *Ancient Records of Egypt*. Chicago, 1906.

Gadd, L. J., *Stones of Assyria*. London, 1936.

Heidel, A., *The Babylonian Genesis*. Chicago, 1954.

Kramer, S. N., *History Begins at Sumer*. New York, 1959.

———*Sumerian Mythology*. New York, 1961.

Layard, A. H., *The Monuments of Nineveh I, II*. London, 1849, 1853.

Luckenbill, D. D., *Ancient Records of Assyria and Babylon*. Chicago, 1926–1927.

Pritchard, J. B., *Ancient Near Eastern Texts Relating to the Old Testament*. Princeton, 1955.

———*The Ancient Near East in Pictures Relating to the Old Testament*. Princeton, 1954.

Schmökel, H., *Kulturgeschichte des alten Orient*. Stuttgart, 1961.

MESOPOTAMIA

Adams, R. M., "Survey of Ancient Watercourses and Settlements in Central Iraq." *Sumer* XIV, Baghdad, 1958.

Buringh, P., "Living Conditions in the Lower Mesopotamian Plain in Ancient Times," *Sumer* XIII, Baghdad, 1957.

Frankfort, H., "Town Planning in Ancient Mesopotamia." *TPR* XXI, 1950.

Kramer, S. N., *The Sumerians*. Chicago, 1963.

Opificius, R., "Befestigungen des Zweistromlandes." *Baghdader Mitteilungen III*, 1964.

Oppenheim, A. L., *Ancient Mesopotamia*. Chicago, 1964.

Pallis, S. A., *The Antiquity of Iraq*. Copenhagen, 1956.

Parrot, A., *Archéologie mésopotamienne I, II*. Paris, 1946–1953.

———*Sumer*. Paris and New York, 1961.

———*Assur*. Paris and New York, 1961.

Roux, G., *Ancient Iraq*. Harmondsworth, 1966.

Saggs, W. F., *The Greatness That Was Babylon*. New York, 1966.

Schmökel, H., *Das Land Sumer*. Stuttgart, 1955.

Schneider, A., *Die Sumerische Tempelstadt*. Essen, 1920.

EGYPT

Aldred, C., *The Egyptians*. New York, 1961.

Badawy, A., *Le dessin architectural chez les anciens Égyptiens*. Cairo, 1948.

———"Orthogonal and Axial Townplanning in Egypt," *Zeitschrift f. ägypt. Sprache u. Altertumskunde*, Vol. 85 (1959), Berlin.

Baedeker, K., *Egypt and the Sudan*, 8th ed. Leipzig, 1929.

Breasted, J. H., *A History of Egypt*. New York, 1964.

Davies, N. de G., "The Townhouse in Ancient Egypt," *MMAS I*, 1929.

Emery, W. B., *Archaic Egypt*. Baltimore, 1961.

Fairman, H. W., "Town Planning in Pharaonic Egypt." *TPR* XX, 1949.

Kees, H., *Ancient Egypt*. Chicago, 1961.

Montet, P., *Everyday Life in Egypt*. New York, 1958.

——— *Eternal Egypt*. New York, 1964.

Moret, A., "Villes neuves et chartes d'immunité dans l'ancien empire égyptien," *Journal Asiatique*, Paris, July-August 1912, March-April 1916, Nov.-Dec. 1917.

Nims, Ch. F., *Thebes of the Pharaohs*. New York, 1965.

Otto, E., *Ägypten*. Stuttgart, 1953.

Pauly, A. T., and Wissowa, G., ed. *Real-Encyclopädie d. klass. Altertums-Wissenschaften. Stuttgart, 1894—present. Articles on Egyptian cities*.

Smith, W. Stevenson, *The Art and Architecture of Ancient Egypt*. Baltimore, 1958.

THE LEVANT

Albright, W. F., *The Archaeology of Palestine*. Baltimore, 1954.

———— *From the Stone Age to Christianity*. New York, 1957.

Baramki, D., *Die Phönizier*. Stuttgart, 1965.

Braidwood, R. J., "Mounds in the Plain of Antioch." *OIP* XLVIII, 1937.

Contenau, G., *La civilisation phénicienne*. Paris, 1949.

Cornfeld, G., *Pictorial Biblical Encyclopedia*. Tel Aviv, 1964.

Gray, J., *The Canaanites*. New York, 1965.

Kenyon, K. M., *Archaeology in the Holy Land*. New York, 1960.

———— *Amorites and Canaanites*. London, 1966.

Noth, M., *The History of Israel*. New York, 1960.

Orlinsky, H. M., *Ancient Israel*. New York, 1954.

Price, I. M., and others, *The Monuments and the Old Testament*. Philadelphia, 1958.

Pritchard, J. B., *Archaeology and the Old Testament*. Princeton, 1958.

Vaux, R. de, *Ancient Israel*. New York, 1961.

Wright, G. E., *Biblical Archaeology*. Philadelphia, 1962.

Yadin, Y., "Hyksos Fortifications and the Battering Ram." *BASOR* CXXXVII, 1955.

———— "Solomon's City Wall and Gate at Gezer." *IEJ* VIII, 1958

ANATOLIA AND THE SYRIAN FOOTHILLS

Akurgal, E., *The Art of the Hittites*. New York, 1962.

———— *Die Kunst Anatoliens*. Berlin, 1961.

Gurney, O. R., *The Hittites*. Baltimore, 1952.

Lloyd, Seton, *Early Anatolia*. Baltimore, 1956.

Mellaart, J., *Earliest Civilizations of the Near East*. New York, 1965.

Naumann, R., *Architektur Kleinasiens*. Tübingen, 1955.

Riemschneider, M., *Die Welt der Hethiter*. Stuttgart, 1954.

Schmökel, H., *Kulturgeschichte des alten Orient*. Stuttgart, 1961.

Vieyra, M., *Hittite Art*. London, 1955.

URARTU

Akurgal, E., "Urartäische Kunst." *Anatolia* IV, 1959.

Barnett, R. D., "Russian Excavations in Armenia." *Excavation Reports Iraq* XII, XIV, XVI, XXI, 1950–1959.

Goetze, A., *Kleinasien*. München, 1957.

Lehmann-Haupt, C. F., *Armenien einst und jetzt*, II. Berlin 1931.

Schmökel, H., *Kulturgeschichte des alten Orient*. Stuttgart, 1961.

ELAM

Hinz, W., *Das Reich Elam*. Stuttgart, 1964.

Porada, E., *The Art of Ancient Iran*. New York, 1965.

IRAN

Ghirshman, R., *Iran*. Baltimore, 1954.

———— *Perse*. Paris, 1964.

Godard, A., *L'art de l'Iran*. Paris, 1962

Herzfeld, E. E., *Iran in the Ancient East*. New York, 1941.

Olmstead, A. T., *History of the Persian Empire*. Chicago, 1948.

Pope, A. U., *A Survey of Persian Art* I, IV. New York, 1938.

Porada, E., *The Art of Ancient Iran*. New York, 1965.

Schmidt, E. F., *Flights over Ancient Iran*. Chicago, 1940.

INDEX

SOURCES OF ILLUSTRATIONS

Numbers refer to figure numbers

Abhandlungen der preussischen Akademie der Wissenschaften, Berlin: 43

Aerofilms Ltd., London: 80

Der alte Orient, Hinrichs (E. Unger, XXVII, 3): 28

Courtesy of the American Museum of Natural History, New York: 1

Anatolian Studies (J. of the British Institute of Archaeology at Ankara),
C. A. Burney, X): 149

Annual of the American Schools of Oriental Research, New Haven
(W. F. Albright, XVII, XXI): 108, 116

Arts Asiatiques, Paris (R. Ghirshman, VIII, X): 152, 154, 155.

Karl Baedeker, *Egypt and the Sudan:* 64, 67, 68

Badawy, *Le dessin architectural chez les anciens Égyptiens*, Service des
Antiquités, Cairo: 63

A. G. Barrois, *Manuel d'archéologie biblique*, I, II, A. Picard: 124

Biblical Archeologist, XVI, New Haven: 96

P. E. Botta and E. Flandin, *Monument de Ninive*, sous la Direction d'une
Commission de l'Institut de France: 9

British Museum, London (D. G. Hogarth, *Carchemish I*): 140; (C. L.
Woolley, *Carchemish II*): 138; (Hogarth & Woolley, *Carchemish III*):
139

British School of Archaeology in Egypt, London (J. C. Quibell, V): 69

British School of Archaeology in Iraq: 29, 30

V. Christian, *Altertumskunde des Zweistromlandes*, Karl W. Hiersemann:
45

I. E. S. Edwards, *Pyramids of Egypt*, Penguin Books, Inc.: 77, 78

W. B. Emery, *Archaic Egypt*, Penguin Books, Inc.: 61, 72, 73, 74

W. B. Emery, *Egypt in Nubia*, Hutchinsin & Co.: 82a, b, c, d

Courtesy of H. W. Fairman: 85

C. S. Fischer, *Excavations at Nippur*, Philadelphia: 23

Forschungen und Fortschritte, Leipzig (E. Unger, VI, XXII): 18, 36

E. Fugmann, *Hama*, Carlsberg Foundation, Copenhagen: 92

L. J. Gadd, *Stones of Assyria*, Chatto & Windus (drawing by Boutcher):
11

P. Geuthner, Paris (M. Dunand, *Fouilles de Byblos* I, II): 103; (R.
Ghirshman, *Fouilles de Sialk près de Kashan*, II): 156; (J. Marquet-
Krause, *Les fouilles de Ay*): 97, 99, 113; (A. Parrot, *Mission archéolo-
gique de Mari* I, II): 53; (C. F. A. Schaeffer, *Ugaritica* I–IV): 110, 111;
(F. Thureau-Dangin, *Til Barsip*): 141; (F. Thureau-Dangin, *Arslan
Tash*): 142; (L. Ch. Watelin and S. Langdon, *Excavations at Kish*): 52

R. Ghirshman, *Perse*, Gallimard: 159, 161, 163

Adrian Grant: 136

Elihu Grant, *Ain Shems Excavations* (Palestine), Haverford College:
109, 115

Harvard University Press, Cambridge (F. S. Starr, *Nuzi* I): 27; (T. J.
Meek, *Excavations at Nuzi* III): 16

S. Hassan, *Excavations at Giza* IV, Government Press, Cairo: 81

Lucien Hervé, Paris: 163

Herzfeld, *Iran in the Ancient East*, Oxford Press: 10

Courtesy of the Hilprecht Collection, University of Jena, Germany: 17

W. Hinz, *Das Reich Elam*, Kohlhammer: 150, 153

U. Hölscher, *Das Grabdenkmal des Königs Chephren*, Hinrichs: 76

Illustrated London News, London (W. B. Emery, June 1958): 83

Iran (J. of the British Institute of Persian Studies), (D. Stronach, I): 160

Israel Exploration Journal, Jerusalem (J. Aharoni and R. Amiran, XXVIII): 98; (Y. Yadin, VIII): 119 a, b, c

Journal of Egyptian Archaeology, London (A. M. Blackman, XIII): 84; (Somers Clarke, VII, VIII): 70, 71, 86

Journal of Near Eastern Studies, II, University of Chicago Press; Courtesy Iraq Museum: 42

Kedem, Jerusalem (E. L. Sukenik, II): 120

Kathleen Kenyon, *Archaeology in the Holy Land*, Ernst Benn: 101, 107

Reconstruction by and courtesy of Mr. J.-Ph. Lauer: 75

C. C. McCown, *Tell en Nasbeh* I, II, New Haven: 122

McGraw-Hill, Inc. (J. Mellaart, *Earliest Civilizations of the Near East*, Thames and Hudson): 126, 127; (Y. Yadin, *The Art of Warfare in Biblical Lands*): 105, 106 a, b, c, d, e, 135

Mansell Collection, London: 12, 158, 165

MATS, Official: 19

The Matson Photoservice, Alhambra, California: 94, 104

Mémoires de la délégation en Perse, Paris (R. Ghirshman, XXXVI): 151

The Metropolitan Museum of Art Bulletin, part II, March 1926, New York: 79

Mitteilungen aus den orientalischen Sammlungen der Berliner Museen, Heft XI–XV (F. von Luschan, K. Humann and R. Koldewey, I–V): 6, 144

Mitteilungen der deutschen Orientgesellschaft, Berlin (O. Puchstein, LXXXIX):15, 133, 134

A. Moret, *Le Nil et la civilization égyptienne*, Éditions de l'Empire: 62

Oriental Institute, University of Chicago: 13, 90, 102, 125

Oriental Institute Communications, University of Chicago: 54, 59

Oriental Institute Publications, University of Chicago: 24, 32, 44, 50, 89, 123, 130

M. von Oppenheim, Tell Halaf, Putnam & Co.: 143

A. Parrot, *Mari*, Ides et Calendes: 47, 48

W. M. F. Petrie, *Illahun, Kahun and Gurob*, London: 65

Philosophical Library (A. Parrot, *Nineveh and the Old Testament*): 49; (A. Parrot, *The Temple of Jerusalem*): 118

Photo Hamikra Baolam: 100, 121

Prof. B. B. Piotrovskii, Hermitage Museum, Leningrad: 146, 148

E. Porada, *The Art of Ancient Iran*, © 1965 by Holle Verlag. Used by permission of Crown Publishers, Inc.: 164

Revue Biblique, Jerusalem (R. de Vaux, LXII): 114

The James de Rothschild Expedition to Hazor, The Hebrew University, Jerusalem: 93

E. F. Schmidt, *Flights over Ancient Iran*, University of Chicago Press: 157, 162

Sendschrift der Deutschen Orient-Gesellschaft, Hinrichs (R. Koldewey, VI): 35

Society of Antiquaries of London: 20, 46, 55, 56, 91, 112

Sumer, Baghdad (S. Smith and Taha Baqir, II): 60

Syria, Paris (F. Hrozny, VIII): 129

R. C. Thompson and R. W. Hutchinson, *A Century of Exploration at Nineveh*, Luzac & Co.: 31

P. Timme, *Tel el Amarna vor der deutschen Ausgrabung im Jahre 1911*, Hinrichs: 66

The maps were drawn under the direction of the author by François Pavageau.